Catch the Wind

The Story of Spiritual Awakening on
The Hebrides Islands

by
Brad Allen

The Story of Spiritual Awakening on
The Hebrides Islands

Printed in the United States of America

ISBN: 1891231-80-4
Library of Congress Control Number: 2002103570

Word Association Publishers
205 Fifth Avenue
Tarentum, Pennsylvania
1-800-827-7903
www.wordassociation.com

Front Cover:
*The childhood home of Duncan Campbell on Achnacree Bay in the Blackcrofts
area. The Ardchattan Church is in the background.*

Dedicated to the memory of

Moryne Craythorne

who had a heart for real revival.

Contents

Preface

The subject of real revival has always intrigued me. Those times when God has suddenly come on a people in great power is something which we should all study, pray for, and desire.

What God did on the Hebrides Islands in 1949-53 was awesome, powerful, and without adequate explanation. Was this a sovereign act of a Sovereign God, or did it happen in response to the prayers of a few people? Who knows? The only place we will ever find a suitable answer to that question is in the hallways of eternity.

Many years ago I read a statement G. Campbell Morgan made about revival. I do not remember the book in which I read it, but Dr. Morgan said revival is a sovereign act of Almighty God, and, since Jesus said, "The wind blows where it will, you hear the sound of it, but cannot tell where it comes from, or where it goes, so is everyone who is born of the Spirit," all we can do is set our sails so that, when the wind of God does blow, we can catch the Wind.

In the years I have been studying the Hebrides Revival, it seems to me that God acted in a sovereign way in those islands. However, there were a few people who had set their sails. When the Wind of God began to blow, these few people were able to "catch the Wind." Among the dear souls who were able to "catch the Wind" were the Rev. Duncan Campbell, Peggy and Christine Smith, Rev. James Murray Mackay, John Smith, Kenneth Macdonald, and Donald Macphail. These are but a few names of many. There were others who had a heart for God, a heart for genuine revival. They were ready to set their sails, and "catch the Wind."

There are so many people I need to thank for the preparation of this manuscript. I would like to thank:

....my wife, Nancy, for her encouragement and determination that I finish this work.

....Moryne Craythrone, who kept after me, as long as she lived, to write this book.

....Johnyne Rees, who carried out her mother's wishes when she didn't have to.

....Special friends, who always prodded me on, prayed for me, and kept me at it.

....Those dear people of the Isle of Lewis, whom it was my privilege to meet; Donald John Smith, Donald and Chrissanna Smith, Donald MacLeod and Cathy, Alex and Mary Murray. Just sitting and talking to these people kindled a fire in my heart that has not gone out.

....Dr. Roy Fish, Professor of Evangelism at Southwestern Baptist Theological Seminary in Ft. Worth, Texas, who "turned me on" to Duncan Campbell, in 1988, by sharing five old audio tapes of this great Scottish preacher.

....The Holy Spirit, who motivated me, convicted me, and opened doors I never dreamed I would be allowed to enter.

As you read these pages, may you think, pray, dare to dream, and set your sails, so that you too, may:

Catch the Wind

CHAPTER ONE

Where the Seagulls Go Wading

In November, 1949, the fire of God fell on the island of Lewis, one of a group of islands known as the Hebrides, off the west coast of Scotland. In all of church history, it is difficult to find a spiritual awakening that was more profound, more wide-spread, or more powerful. The power of the Living God fell on these islands in such a fashion that to read about this awakening is like reading a foreign language one does not understand.

Of all the places for the power of God to come, the Hebrides Islands are some of the most unlikely and most unique in all the world. I have found that many people not only do not know much about the Hebrides Islands, many have never heard of these islands.

The Hebrides Islands consist of two groups of islands off the northwest coast of Scotland. The group of islands closest to the mainland of Scotland is called the Inner Hebrides. The other group, located farther west, is called the Outer Hebrides.

The main islands of the Inner Hebrides are Skye, Canna, Bum, Eigy, Muck, Coll, Tiree, Lismore, Mull, Ulva, Staffa, Iona, Kenera, Calonsay, Oronsay, Scarba, Jura, Islay, and Gigha.

The principal islands of the Outer Hebrides are Lewis with Harris, North Uist, South Uist, Barra, Benbecula, Shiants, St. Kilda, and the Flannan Isles. This chain of islands called the Outer Hebrides stretches for a distance of 130 miles from Barra in the south to the Butt of Lewis in the north. These islands vary in width from thirty miles to less than one mile.

The land of the Hebrides is harsh and rugged. Much of the land is rocky and mountainous. Of the total area of 2,812 square miles, only some 300 square miles is cultivable. The climate is wet, with fierce winds blowing in from the Atlantic Ocean much of the time. From the westernmost island, St. Kilda, there is nothing west of Kilda except ocean until you reach the shores of Newfoundland.

The Hebrides are barren islands. There are few trees except on the islands of Lewis, Skye, Jura, and Mull. The people of the Hebrides live by the sea. It is not only their home, but also their livelihood. It controls much of their lives.

Before the construction of airstrips, planes landed on the island of Barra on the beach. Twice a day, as the tide would sweep out, planes could land on the solid pack of cockleshells. Pilots claimed it was safe to land when the seagulls would go wading. [1]

There are almost 500 islands in the chain known as the Hebrides, of which about 100 are inhabited. Many of the islands are uninhabited because of the severe conditions of human existence. Because of the severity of existence, and the lack of opportunity in the work force, population decline has been a major problem for the Hebrides for decades. The total population of the Island of Skye dropped from 23,000 to 9,000 across the last half of the 20th Century. There is a saying in Skye, "Our imports are various; our exports are young men and young women." [2]

In the period between World War I and World War II, emigration took a heavy toll on the islands. In fact, the number of people leaving South Uist and Lewis during this time period required the presence of an Atlantic Ocean liner in a local port. [3]

The people of the Hebrides are known as friendly, outgoing, gregarious people. During my trip to the Hebrides, I discovered the most kind, gracious people I have ever met. They were most willing to open their homes, invite you to eat with them. On a few occasions, while walking down the street looking for something, I would ask a passerby where a certain place was. The person would start to give directions, and then say, "Just follow me. I will show you where it is." The people of the Hebrides have known their share of poverty, at times, even hunger. However, even in the midst of all their problems, they have a peace about them, the peace of a people of a classless society. They live in a land, "where no man commands another. They can risk friendliness, and they do." [4]

But, times change for the people of the Hebrides, as it changes for other people. One crofter (farmer) said, "We belong to this place. I'm a Gaelic-speaking man; we all had the Gaelic once. Och, but now we're growing few, and our tongue is being lost, and the language holds the tales, and the tales hold the knowledge of the old ways and the old days, of holy and unholy things [5]

Today, it is rare to find a family in the Hebrides Islands that is not connected to the other nations, with relatives who have emigrated to Canada, the United States, or Australia. The main reason for the large emigration of young people has been the lack of economic opportunity. The two main sources of work on the islands are crofting (farming) and the fishing industry. The main crops grown on the small amount of acres that are arable are potatoes, turnips, barley, and oats. Across the years, black oats rather than white oats have been grown on the Hebrides, because the black oats could withstand the fierce winds better than the white oats. Toward the end of the 1800's, potatoes were introduced to the Hebrides. The people found them easy to grow, but they did not care for their taste, and they refused to eat them. Gradually, potatoes took precedence over other crops. Today, the residents of the Hebrides rely on the raising of sheep and cattle, distilling whiskey, quarrying slate, extracting alginates from seaweed and the manufacturing of woolen garments. Today, the name, Harris Tweed, is known all over the world.

One of the unique features of the Island of Lewis is the "Blackhouse." For centuries, the people lived in these thatched-roofed houses, constructed to withstand the cold and fierce winds. These houses were long, with rounded ends, having the cattle under the same roof with a partition between the cattle and the living quarters. The name, "blackhouse" dates back to the last part of the 1800's when modern houses began to be built. The modern houses were called, "whitehouses." Modern houses began to be built in large numbers at the close of World War II when the young men and women began to return from the war. The Blackhouses were built as a combination byre, barn, and home in the same tradition of the "long houses" which have existed in Northern Europe for well over 1000 years. The Blackhouses did not have chimney or windows and were built entirely of materials that could be found locally; stone, turf, thatch of oat, barley or grass.

The living room in the Blackhouse had a fire in the center of the floor. The smoke had to find its way out of the room through the thatched roof. The phrase, "gather round the fire", was taken quite literally in the Hebrides. The earthen floor in the Blackhouse was warmer than cement. The walls were four feet thick, and were doubled. In the cavity between the double walls were placed small stones or dirt for insulation. The roof was constructed of turf laid on wooden rafters, covered with reeds, grass or heather. A fishing net or chicken wire was spread over the thatched roof, then all of this was anchored by large stones to keep the wind from blowing the roof away.

Today, there is a preserved Blackhouse in the village of Arnol, on the Island of Lewis. It is made up of byre, barn, living room and bedroom. Box-beds were used in the bedroom to protect the sleeper from drafty winds and leaking roofs. The byre gave the cattle, sheep and chickens a place to stay out of the weather. The barn provided a place to store hay for the animals.

The history of the Hebrides Islands is long and interesting. These islands were known by Ptolemy and Pliny early in the Christian era. The islands were first occupied by the Celtic tribes, and, then, in the sixth century, they were occupied by the Norse. In fact, of all the explanations for the name, Hebrides, the most likely explanation for the naming of the islands came during the occupation of the Norse. In the Norse language, the three words, HAV BRED EY, means "isles on the edge of the sea." [6] The Norse invaders, who were called Vikings, were divided into two groups; the Fionn-Ghoill, the White Foreigners, who came from Norway and Sweden and the Dubh-Ghoill, the Black Foreigners who came from Denmark. [7] The number of centuries of Norse occupation of the Hebrides has left its mark on these islands to this day. The number of place names that still bear the mark of the Norse language are plentiful. The dals (vales), bhals (hills), bhats (water) are all Norse names. Also, you will find many of the villages with sta, bost, or shader added to the name of a previous occupant.

The Isle of Lewis and the rest of the Western Isles were ceded to Scotland in 1266 A. D. by the Treaty of Perth. King Magnus II of Norway made this treaty with Alexander III of Scotland, renouncing all claim to the Hebrides Islands. The islands were held by local chieftains until 1346 A.D., when John MacDonald of Islay proclaimed an independent rule over the islands. His rule, and that of his family, continued until 1748 A.D.

One of the unique features of the people of the Hebrides Islands has been their deep belief in witches, ghosts, and other superstitions. Across the centuries, these beliefs were deeply imbedded in the thoughts of the people. It was not until the coming of belief in Jesus Christ that these superstitious beliefs were abandoned.

According to Gaelic superstition, witches come to a house only from the north. In Celtic legend, a ford is the favorite meeting place for ghosts.

On many of the islands are abandoned fortresses or forts. Many people believe these abandoned forts become the home of the "little people" and they must be treated with respect. The little people, made up of fairies, brownies and elves are neither omnipotent nor malevolent. They have large, dangerous friends, their fairy dogs. These dogs are big and black, with blazing eyes. These little people also have water horses. These horses live in dark pools of water from which they emerge to pursue and injure human beings. These water horses can also turn into human form and mix with or marry human beings.

One of the most unusual, intriguing stories of the superstitions of the islands has to do with the ancient pagan sea-god, Shony. Shony was the giver of seaware (seaweed). At night, on Hallowtide, someone was chosen to wade into the sea at night clutching a cup of ale. This ale was offered to the god, Shony, with these words, "Shony, I give you this cup of ale, hoping that you will be so kind as to send us plenty of seaware for enriching our ground." [8]

The people of the Hebrides are an educated, fun-loving people. They are happy people, who are full of song, poetry and sport. They have a great sense of humor and do not live in stress with the confines of modern-day society. Time means very little to the people of the Hebrides. A writer who was touring the Hebrides asked a man what time it was. The man replied, "August, Sir." [9]

One traveler in the Hebrides was impatient when his bus driver seemed to be in no hurry to be off. A lady on the bus said to the traveler, "I can see you are a stranger. You'll not be knowing the Gaelic, 'mo thogairi.' It means, 'I don't care, or it makes no difference.' That is the operating principles of the buses of Skye, mo thogairi." [10]

The love of good times and sport is inbred in Hebridean life. When the Highland Games begin in a town, a band of pipers usually begin the games with rousing songs played as only bagpipes can play them. The games consist of the tossing of cabers, which are poles twenty feet long; blowing pipes, throwing fifty pound weights over crossbars ten feet high, and throwing the hammer, which has been described as a "cannon ball on a stick." [11]

Another form of entertainment in the Hebrides is the "ceilidh" (pronounced kay-lee). A ceilidh is a party held in someone's home. At this party, they sing, play the bagpipes, tell stories, and tell jokes. The ceilidh may go on well past midnight.

In October, 2001, my wife and I had the privilege of traveling to some of the Hebrides Islands. We got to visit the Isle of Lewis, and the Isle of Skye. I would like to take the reader on a brief journey through the Hebrides Islands. We shall first travel through the Inner Hebrides and finish our trip on the Outer Hebrides.

THE ISLE OF ISLAY

Islay is the southern-most island of the Hebrides. Its principal town is Bowmore. On the Island of Islay, you will find round churches, built in that fashion for a purpose. The churches are round in shape so the devil will not be able to find a corner in which to hide.

As we journey to this island, we are coming to view castles or mountains. We have come to Islay to see, tucked in a wooded area, a beautiful Celtic cross carved almost 1200 years ago to the glory of Jesus Christ. This cross was placed by Celts called, "Scotti", who came from Christian Ireland in the Sixth Century. These 'Scotti" came to Islay to spread the message of Jesus Christ in the pagan Highlands and the islands.

For several centuries the MacDonald clan, which means, 'noble house", in Gaelic, ruled the island of Islay. The MacDonald clan lost Islay to the Campbells of Argyll in 1614.

THE ISLE OF JURA

Although close by to the Island of Islay, the Island of Jura differs greatly from that of Islay. Islay is green and grassy, while Jura is dark and mountainous. The name, Jura, is of Norse origin, and means, "deer island." The island is rightly named, for the only numerous animals on the island are deer.

On the southern end of Jura stand three imposing mountains, rising from the sea. The tallest of the three, Beinn Siantaidh, "sacred mountain", stands 2,477 feet above sea level.

THE ISLE OF IONA

Iona a one of the smaller islands in the Inner Hebrides. The entire island covers only three square miles. This tiny island is famous because it saw the birth of Christianity in Western Scotland. The Irish Saint, Columba, established the first church and monastery in Scotland on this minute island.

There is an ancient legend about Columba and his monks on the island of Iona. Before they built the abbey, they lived in huts and tried to build for their worship a small chapel. The walls would not stand until one of the monks, Odhrain, let himself be buried alive in the foundation of the chapel. Columba dug him up after three days to have a last look at him. Odhrain revived and declared that neither heaven nor hell were exactly as Christian teaching described them. He was promptly reburied for his heresy. [12]

Before 1200 A.D., the chapel and graveyard, "reilig odhrain", were the most revered sites in Scotland. In this old graveyard lie Duncan and Macbeth, along with forty-six other Scottish kings, four Irish, and eight Norwegian.

THE ISLE OF TIREE
Sailing through the Sound of Sleat and the Kyle (strait) of Lochalsh, we come to the small Island of Tiree. It is said that you can recognize the walk of the islanders of Tiree anywhere by the curious angled slant of their walk, caused by so often fighting to stay upright against the wild western gales.

THE ISLE OF SKYE
Skye is the largest island of the Inner Hebrides. It measures fifty miles from north to south and as much as twenty-five miles across. My trip to the Isle of Skye was one of the most impressive sights during my trip to the Hebrides. Skye is lush, green, full of trees, grass and many different varieties of plants. I drove to the south end of Skye to the small village of Ardvasar. Along the road were large trees, with wild fern growing in abundance under the trees.

For centuries the MacDonald Clan ruled the island of Skye. For generations their castle was at Duntulin, on the northern cape of the island, but, driven by the cold north winds of the Arctic Ocean, the clan moved to the southern end of Skye where they built a new castle. Here the grass is green, and flowers bloom. It is typical that the two main villages on the southern end of the island are named Armadale and Ardvasar. The first town's name is Norse, and the second is Celtic. The Norsemen held Skye for many years until a Celtic warrior, Somerled, captured it from them. Both the Norse and the Celts have left their mark on the Island of Skye. The name, Skye, may come from two Norse words, SKY EY, meaning, "cloud island."

One of the most famous landmarks on the Island of Skye is Dunvegan Castle, and the most famous family or clan on the island are the Macleods. Dunvegan Castle stands on a sheer wall of rock. A castle has stood at that spot for more than 1000 years. This castle has been the stronghold of the Clan Macleod and has been lived in by this same family for over 700 years. [13]

The real importance of the clan system has been gone from Scotland since Bonnie Prince Charlie failed to restore the Stuarts to the throne of Britain in 1745-46. It was during this time that clans rose against the Hanovers of England. When defeat came, the wearing of the kilt and the carrying of weapons were banned. This was the time of the infamous "Clearances", the clearance of clansmen and the substitution of sheep when shipload after shipload of Scottish Highlanders sailed for the United States, Nova Scotia, Australia, and New Zealand. In fact, in Nova Scotia descendants still speak Gaelic and, on occasion, wear kilts.

It is on the Island of Skye that we meet a famous lady in Hebridean history. Flora MacDonald is the young heroine who some say rowed Bonnie Prince Charlie to a hiding place on the Island of Skye. More reliable history books tell us that she recruited five husky Highlanders to do the rowing. Flora dressed the Prince as her maid and was almost discovered by the Redcoats because Prince Charlie carried his petticoats in such an awkward manner, since he was so unaccustomed to them.

It is now time for us to move from the Inner Hebrides to the Outer Hebrides. We will look at six principal islands of the Outer Hebrides. When looking at spiritual awakening that took place in the Hebrides Islands, it is important to look at the Outer Hebrides, for it was here that the Holy Spirit of God fell in such great power during the revival of 1949-53.

THE ISLE OF BARRA

Barra is a small island approximately ten miles long and eight miles wide. On Barra, as on the other islands, time means little. The people have not been caught up in the world of schedules and daytimers. A Mr. MacPherson said to an impatient visitor to the island, "The only watch we study here is the sun and the tides."

The Island of Barra is predominantly Roman Catholic, while the northern islands are Church of Scotland. One reporter heard an organ playing on the Island of Barra and recalled that among the music-scorning Calvinists of the northern islands, the organ was known as "a kist of whistles", as ungodly as the bagpipes, those 'black sticks of the devil." A Mrs. Sinclair of Barra said, "It's just that they are terribly holy in the northern islands." [14]

The industry of Barra has increased over the past several decades. Most of this increase has to do with the work of the Highlands and Islands Development Board, an organization which is investing much time and money in the development of industry.

There are small businesses which produce frames for eye-glasses, perfumes and electronic controls. Each product made on the Island of Barra is chosen because it is small and light, to avoid high freight costs.

On the northwestern coast of Barra is a mile-long beach called TRAIGH MHOR. This beach is made up entirely of cockleshells. A company gathers these shells, pulverizes them into grit for poultry food. This supply of cockleshells seems endless.

Another industry on Barra is the collection and processing of seaweed. The seaweed is dried, pulverized, bagged, then shipped to chemical plants on the mainland. From this seaweed, a variety of products are made; thickening for tooth paste, stabilizing ice cream, molding dental impressions, coating pills, making medical dressings, and textiles.

One traveler found Roderick, Barra's piper, who made his living manufacturing reeds for bagpipes. This is a very intricate work, and requires a fine ear. Roderick cut the reeds from Spanish cane and they were in demand all over Scotland. [15]

Anytime you meet an islander from Barra, you can always

expect some comment on the weather. One traveler on Barra met Archie Beg (Little Archie), and, as Gaelic ritual requires, Archie Beg said, "I do not like this dry, east wind. It brings dirt from the mainland and is unhealthy. We are made to live in moisture and do not care for the cold, bright day." [16]

THE ISLE OF ERISKAY
Eriskay is a tiny island, no more than two miles in any direction. This tiny island has gained
its fame because it was here that Bonnie Prince Charlie Stuart made his first landing from the French brig in an ill-fated attempt to win the British throne in 1745. The white, sandy beach of Eriskay is still called, "Prince's Beach."

Eriskay is a Roman Catholic island and has a population of about 200. The church on the island was built as a memorial to the work of its most beloved priest, Father Allan MacDonald, who is buried in the little cemetery. There is a story that is told on Eriskay of the solitary protestant who once lived on Eriskay. When he died, no one knew where he should be buried. At last it was decided to give him the place of honor, next to Father Allan. And there he lies today.

THE ISLE OF SOUTH UIST
South Uist is a large island, about twenty miles long. You can see fields of oats and barley as you make your way across the island.

South Uist gains its fame from the fact it is the birthplace of Flora MacDonald who led Prince Charlie in his escape from British soldiers to the Island of Skye. Flora dressed the Prince as her maidservant, but he was nearly discovered because he carried his petticoats so awkwardly.

THE ISLE OF BENBECULA
Benbecula, "the mountain of the fords" (as Benbecula means in Gaelic) is a relatively small island that sits between South Uist and North Uist. Today a half-mile long bridge links Benbecula to South Uist. In years gone by one could travel between South Uist and Benbecula by horse and carriage during low tide.

The building of an air strip has probably changed Benbecula

more than anything. In the old days it was claimed that the journey from Stornoway to Barra was as long as the trip to New York. A traveler had to sail to the mainland of Scotland, and then sail back to the islands.

Benbecula is equally divided between Roman Catholic and Protestants. This island is, indeed, the meeting place of the two faiths.

THE ISLE OF NORTH UIST

North Uist lies south of the large island of Lewis. It lies three to four miles north of the Island of Benbecula. Across the years this distance could be traveled by horse and carriage or by lorry during low tide.

North Uist is rich in prehistoric remains. There are remains of earth houses that date from the Iron Age. There are brochs (round towers) that were occupied during the days of the Roman Empire, and there are chambered cairns of Neolithic times covered by huge piles of stones. [17]

THE ISLE OF LEWIS

Lewis is the largest island of the Hebrides. It is commonly called, "the long island." The length of Lewis was often expressed in ancient times as being from Tigh nan Cailleachan Dubha an Uig, House of the Black-robed Women in Uig, to Tigh Mhaoilruibhe ann a' Nis, Mulvay's house in Ness. Back across the years, the island's official name was Lewis on Harris. The southern part of the island is the area of Harris, and the northern part of the island is Lewis. Although they are geographically one island, Harris and Lewis are split by clan affiliation, county allegiance, and common consent. The two areas differ in so many ways. Lewis is low and wet. Black bog covers most of its surface, but it has a relatively large population along its shores. Harris is beautiful with its mountains, shining sea lochs and hidden dells with earth and life.

The Lewis and Harris people share a common ancestry. They both came from a Norse Clan named Leod that inhabited the island. Two sons of Leod, therefore named Macleod, each founded a tribe; Torquil, the Macleods of Lewis and Tormod, the Macleods of Harris. [18]

It is thirty-six miles from Tarbert on Harris, or southern end of the island, to Stornoway on the Lewis, or northern end of the island. The road between these two towns travels over Clisham, the highest mountain in the Outer Hebrides.

The industry of Lewis on Harris is mainly the herring industry and the making of Harris Tweed. The weaving of Harris Tweed is world-famous. It is entirely a cottage industry. The yarn is woven, usually by men, on hand looms in the houses, after being processed and spun at one of the large mills in Stornoway or Tarbert.

The standards for Harris Tweed are very strict. It must be made from pure virgin wool, produced in Scotland, spun, dyed and finished in the Outer Hebrides and hand-woven by the islanders in their own homes. It is a fabric of rare excellence. To insure that the cloth is genuine, the buyer should look for the certification mark stamped on the cloth at three-yard intervals in the mills. The certification mark is a patee cross surmounting an orb, with the words, "Harris Tweed."

One of the weavers was pedaling along on his loom, and said with a smile, "Stupid, isn't it? A motor would be running this loom just as well as my tired old legs. Ach, but then it would not be Harris Tweed." [19]

It is most interesting where the weavers get their dye for the Harris Tweed. First, they soak the yarn in stale urine to set the thread. The dyes come from the following; peat root makes a mousy brown, iris root makes a pale yellow, bog myrtle a deep yellow, heather tips make a light green, rock lichen makes a rusty orange, the yellow iris makes a bluish gray, the nettle makes a light blue, the root of the water lily makes a black, and the madder, imported from France, makes a red.

In the cemetery at Rodel, the town on the southern tip of the island of Lewis on Harris, is buried a unique character in the history of the Hebrides. "Msiri Nighean Aiastrir Ruaidh" (Mary Macleod) was born in 1588. She was the nurse to the Macleod family, and was famous as a poetess. Mary lived to the age of 105. In her old age she walked with a silver-headed cane and was fond of a pinch of snuff. She was once banished by the chief of the Macleods because she composed a song which offended him. Later she wrote another song to placate the chief and was recalled from exile. The story goes that, on her deathbed, Mary Macleod asked to be buried face down as a sign of repentance for having given in to the Macleod chieftain against her better judgment. [20]

One of the unique features on the Island of Lewis is the prehistoric circle of stones found at Callanish. This group of stones rivals Stonehenge in the number of stones. These stones were set between 3,000 and 4,000 years ago. The Callanish Stones, or Fir-Bhreige Chalanais, as they are called in Gaelic, are arranged in the form of a cross with a circle at its juncture. It is the form of a Celtic cross. Yet, they were set up 2000 years before the cross became a symbol of Christianity. Scholars believe these stones may be a prehistoric calendar, or, they may mark the site of a temple where the early Celts worshiped Bel, the Sun god. The Callanish Stones are set on top of a hill toward the south end of the Isle of Lewis, with hills and moorland to the north, and a loch to the south. The day I was there, the wind was blowing in from the sea, and, these forty-two stones that range from three and one-half feet to fifteen and one-half feet in height stood as silent sentinels over a civilization that has been silent for thousands of years. I stood there and wondered why these stones came to be called by the people of Lewis, Na Fir Bhreige, "The Deceitful Men."

One of the interesting episodes from the history of Lewis happened in 1918. William Lever, a multi-millionaire, bought the Island of Lewis. He was prepared to spend 25 million dollars to convert the island into a thriving commercial center. But many of the island's crofters (farmers) preferred the old ways, and refused to cooperate with Lever. His plans failed.

Among Lever's creations are Lux and Lifebuoy soap. Today his name lives on in the world of stock markets and supermarkets under the name of Lever Brothers.

Lewis and Harris are both strongly protestant. The people of this island are very strict in the observance of their faith in Jesus Christ. The Sabbath is not lightly broken, nor seldom even bent. Today, on Lewis and Harris airplanes do not fly on Sunday, buses do not run, taxis are unavailable, and most businesses are closed.

At the extreme northern end of the Island of Lewis is the Butt of Lewis. Here stands the 14th Century Kirk (Church) of Eoropie. In ancient days, pilgrimages were taken to this sight for the cure of the mentally ill. The mentally-ill patient was walked around the church seven times, then was left bound hand and foot inside the church all night. If he or she was not cured by morning, the case was considered hopeless.

The sons and daughters of the Hebrides are scattered across the world. However, you can remove an islander from the Hebrides, but you can never remove the Hebrides from an islander. As an anonymous man from the Island of Skye wrote in far-off Canada:
> From the lone shieling of the misty island
> Mountains divide us, and the waste of seas;
> Yet still the blood is strong, the heart is Highland,
> And we in dreams behold the Hebrides.

It was into these wild, beautiful islands, with their beautiful lochs, serene dells, rocky mountains, and relentless gales of wind that the wind of the Holy Spirit blew in 1949-53. A spiritual awakening unmatched in all of Christian history unfolded in these quaint islands in mighty force.

Jesus once said, "The wind blows where it will. You hear the sound of it, but you cannot tell where it comes from, and where it goes; so is every one that is born of the Spirit." (John 3:8)

What a story! The Hebrides, which used to be known as the place where the seagulls go wading, now has become known as the place where Almighty God went striding across the land in awesome power.

> Not until the loom is silent,
>   And the shuttles cease to fly,
> Will God unroll the canvas
>   And explain the reason why.
> The dark threads are as needful
>   In the weaver's skillful hand
> As the threads of gold and silver
>   In the pattern He has planned.

CHAPTER TWO

From Sword Dance to Salvation

It is a bit strange to single out any one person in the Hebrides Awakening because what happened there was totally of God. God came in all His power and brought revival to those islands. However, when you speak of the Hebrides Revival, you are drawn immediately to the principal person whom God used in that movement. His name was Duncan Campbell. Campbell was a Scottish Highlander preacher whom God used as His human instrument.

Duncan Campbell was born in 1898 in the Argyllshire area of Scotland. I had the privilege of visiting this area about six miles north of Oban, Scotland. It is one of the most beautiful areas I have ever seen, lush foliage, the land covered with green grass, mountains and water.

Campbell came from sturdy, hard-working Highland stock. His father was Hugh Campbell, who pursued a career as a stone mason. Hugh Campbell's father had bought a small farm on the shores of a sea loch called Achnacree Bay. The house where he moved and raised his family is still standing today, and is occupied by Duncan Campbell's nephew, Donald Campbell. The small farm is located in what was called the "Black Crofts' area. It received this name many years before the Campbell family came here. Before this land was settled, a wealthy landowner used it as a penitentiary area. He sent sheep-stealers and those who had defaulted on their taxes to this area with no more than a spade, and they began farming the Black Crofts area.

When Hugh Campbell began to look around for a wife, he found a lovely young lass named Jane Livingston. It is said that Jane had deep brown eyes, a high brow, full lips and wavy, brunette hair. Jane was born on the nearby island of Lismore. The Livingstones of Lismore became a very famous family. Part of the Livingstones lived on the small island of Ulva. There, in a very poor home, a boy, David Livingstone, was born. This was the David Livingstone who spent his life as a missionary in Central Africa, and, today, his body lies buried in Westminister Abbey in London.

Hugh Campbell and his bride, Jane, set up housekeeping in the Blackcrofts. This name had nothing to do with the color, black, but referred to the character of those who had first settled that area many years before.

The Campbell croft (farm) was named Camus-liath, "the grey estuary." Hugh and Jane Campbell had a total of ten children. Duncan was the fifth child born into the family. As was the custom, Duncan was baptized into the Ardchattan Parish Church. The name, Ardchattan, comes from two Gaelic words; ard, which means, "a high point", and cattan, which means, "little cat." It is believed that Cattan was the name of an Irish Pict who came to this area early in its history. He was possibly a monk. What a beautiful setting for this old church. The day I visited this area, I stopped about two miles down the road east of the church. A man was in his yard working on his car. I asked him if he knew where the Ardchattan Church was. He said he was not sure, but there was a church about two miles down the road. I asked him if it was an old church. He said, "No. It is only about 200 years old." You can stand outside the house where Duncan Campbell was born and raised and look across Achnacree Bay. Achnacree means, "the field of the tree." The Ardchattan Church is setting on the banks of Achnacree Bay northeast of the house. It is an absolutely stunning view. The day I was in the Blackcrofts area, it was Sunday. My wife and I attended morning worship service at the Ardchatten Church. It is a large church, I would estimate it would seat 500 people. That morning there were 32 people present. After the service, I visited with the Minister and found out one interesting feature about the church. All the pews face the front of the auditorium, except for two rows of pews in the center. These two rows sit at the ninety degree angle to the pulpit, with a long table sitting between the pews. The purpose of these two pews and the table: This is the Lord's Table. Many years ago, when it was time for Communion, those who felt worthy to take Communion would leave their pews and make their way to this partitioned area of the Lord's Table. There they would take Communion. The Minister told me there were only five churches in Scotland that still had this arrangement of the Lord's Table.

When Duncan Campbell was three years of age, an unusual and far-reaching event took place in the Blackcroft area. Two young ladies came to Benderloch, a village about four miles from the Campbell home. These two young ladies began to preach in halls, schools, barns, and any other place they could find to hold a crowd of people. These young ladies called themselves, "pilgrims." They were missionaries with the Faith Mission which was headquartered in Edinbrough. Their coming caused quite a commotion in the area, for women preachers were unheard of. Perhaps because of the novelty of the idea, people came to hear what these two young ladies had to say. They reminded people of a preacher of many, many years before. John Campbell, no relation to Duncan Campbell, came to this area and began to preach salvation in Jesus Christ by grace alone. He became known as the Bard of Benderloch. He preached for forty years in a cave at Leaig. John Campbell had converted a natural cave into a place of worship. He placed seats around the curve of the cave, and, from a small table, John Campbell, the Bard of Benderloch, preached the good news of Jesus Christ to crowds of people. When I was in this area, I inquired about this cave, and found that the cave had been destroyed during highway construction.

Hugh Campbell, and his wife, Jane, attended the meetings of these two young ladies. One of the young ladies, Maggie Campbell, had been laboring for the Lord for eleven years in the Highlands of Scotland. It was her habit to stand and speak about Jesus Christ. With tears streaming down her face, she would urge people to give their lives to Jesus Christ. One night Hugh Campbell, his wife, Jane, and their eldest son were saved and became followers of Jesus Christ. They began to attend church, and, also to follow the custom of the Highlands; to have regular family devotions. Hugh Campbell became the Precentor at the Ardchattan Church. In the Church of Scotland, the music director, or music leader is called the Precentor. Hugh Campbell would take his place each Sunday morning in the lower pulpit at the church, and announce the Psalm they would sing. It is interesting to note that, even today, in the Hebrides Islands, they only sing Psalms, with no musical instruments.

Because Hugh Campbell left for his work as a stone mason so early in the morning, Jane would lead her children in family devotions. Duncan Campbell said the family would rise at 5:30 A.M., go out to feed the horses, come back in the house and have a breakfast of tea and oatcakes, then the time from 6:30 A.M. to 7:30 A.M. was given to singing, prayer and reading the Scriptures This occurred each morning. This made a deep impression on Duncan Campbell's life. Over and over again, through the years, he would remark about the daily devotions his mother led. Duncan Campbell also said that when the children would leave for school, his mother would sit down by the fireplace, throw her apron over her head, and meet with her Savior. Duncan Campbell grew up in a home where prayer had a prominent place. For all of his life, that one hour, from 6:30 until 7:30 in the morning, made a lasting impression upon Campbell's life. Quietness in the farmhouse, in order that the family might listen to God, to give God the opportunity to speak to them.

Duncan Campbell was described by one of his brothers as a "wee rascal" with bright red hair and extremely independent. The brother said that Duncan would risk the wrath of anyone to defend his pals.

When Duncan Campbell was fifteen years old, he became known in the community as Am Piobaire Ruadh, "the Red Piper." He would go around the area playing the bagpipes and performing the Scottish sword dance. One night he went to a meeting house to play the bagpipes at a local dance. He took along his bagpipes and two swords for the performing of the sword dance. This was the night that God, in His mercy, saved Duncan Campbell. He was playing the old Scottish tune, "The Green Hills of Tyrol", when, suddenly, without warning, deep conviction seized him. A question kept nagging at his soul, "Is this all that life has to offer a young fellow?"

Duncan realized he had a praying father and mother. He knew they were deeply burdened for him. He found himself dwelling, not on the Green Hills of Tyrol, but thinking about the hill of Calvary. He found himself thinking about Jesus Christ dying on the cross. Why was He there? What had He ever done to deserve this? Suddenly, Duncan felt he was quite responsible for the death of Christ on the cross. When he finished playing the tune on his bagpipes, he went to the chairman of the dance, who happened to be a minister, and told him, "I am sorry, but I have to go home.'

The minister/chairman asked Duncan, "What is wrong? Are you sick?"

Duncan replied, "I am fine in my body, but it is my soul that is troubled. I have just discovered that I am lost and on my way to hell."

The minister replied, "Don't worry about it. You will get over it."

But, Duncan Campbell never got over it as long as he lived.

This night changed his life forever.

Duncan left the dance with a friend of his. For some reason this other boy was also deeply concerned about his own soul. The two boys fell into step together, walking down a narrow, country road talking about their lost condition and the way of salvation. They reached a junction in the road where they had to part. The other boy asked Duncan, "What are we going to do?" Duncan replied, "I don't know about you, but I am going home to get right with God tonight."

The other boy said, "I think I will wait awhile." That other boy waited and waited until he grew to manhood, became a successful businessman, and, then, in old age he was taken to a nursing home to die, LOST. In the nursing home, he was questioned about his spiritual state and was urged to accept Christ. That other boy who was now an old, unsaved man said, "Speak no more to me on that matter. I settled it the night Duncan was saved. [1]

Duncan Campbell started walking home. He passed a meeting home where the lights were on. This was a memorial meeting hall that had been built years before at Alt-na-mara in memory of John Campbell, the Bard of Benderloch, who had preached for forty years in a cave. Alt-na-mara means, "The stream by the sea." When Duncan came to this meeting hall, it was 11:00 at night. He realized church was going on. He had been away from home for several weeks working, and did not know that two lady pilgrims of the Faith Mission were conducting services in the area. Duncan slipped up close to the door of the meeting hall and listened. He heard someone praying. It was his father, Hugh Campbell. He was pouring his heart out for the church and his own family. Duncan went into the meeting hall. He was dressed in the garb of a piper, carrying a set of bagpipes and two swords. He placed the bagpipes and swords on the back pew, walked down the aisle and took a seat by his father. His father looked over at him and said, "I'm glad to see you here, Laddie, I'm glad to see you here." [2]

The two young pilgrims who were in the parish conducting the mission were Mary Graham from the Isle of Skye and Jessie Mowat from Aberdeen. A few minutes after Duncan sat down in the meeting, Mary Graham rose to her feet and quoted a verse from the Bible, "God speaketh once, yea twice, yet man perceiveth it not." (Job

33:14). Duncan said he knew that God was speaking to him, but he was so afraid he would cause a disturbance in the meeting that he rose, picked up his bagpipes and swords and left the meeting.

Again, Duncan started walking home. On the way home that night, Duncan continually fell to the country road on his knees, crying out to God for mercy. He said he did not know how many times he did this on the walk home. He was so distressed in his soul that he was afraid the ground would open and he would fall into hell. (3) He finally reached home, that house sitting on the banks of Achnacree Bay, about 2:00 A.M. When he walked into the house, he found his dear mother on her knees by the kitchen fire. She had been unable to go to the church meeting that night. Friends had come to the home earlier that day and were staying overnight. Duncan went to his mother and told her what was happening to him. He told her how distressed he was in his heart. Jane Campbell looked at her son, and said, "Your cousins are in your bedroom, but I will soon get a bed ready for you. But I would say this to you, laddie, go out to the barn and tell God what you have told me.' Duncan took her advice. He went to the barn, saw a pile of straw prepared for the horses for the next morning. He fell on his knees in the straw, and, years later, Duncan Campbell could still remember the prayer he prayed that night, "O, God, I know not how to come. I know not what to do, but, my God, I'm coming now. Oh, have mercy on me." Duncan Campbell said, "In that moment I felt myself to have been born again." 4 God swept into Duncan Campbell's life and he was gloriously saved. A miracle had taken place.

Duncan Campbell said of this experience, "Is it not true that a born-again Christian is a supernatural being? A supernatural being who has had a supernatural experience . Not for one single moment since that night have I ever, on any occasion, doubted the work God did in my heart. It was real. It was definite, and it was supernatural." 5

Throughout the rest of his life, Duncan Campbell lived in the reality of his salvation experience. He made more than a decision. He had an encounter with the Living God. One predominant note in his preaching in years to come was, "Is God real to you?" His cry can be heard in a sermon, "We are living in a day, particularly in the field of evangelism, when everything is real, but God. Organization, real! Activity, real! Evangelism, real! Decision, real! Yes, even decisions can be real to you without God. Oh, tell me, is God the supreme reality in your experience?" 6

The young, fifteen-year-old "red piper" has come to a major crossroads in his life. Little did he know that night, kneeling in the pile of straw in the barn that he would one day see the fire of God fall on many of the Hebrides Islands. BUT, something more is needed for young Duncan Campbell. He is saved, but the mighty power of God in his life is a secret he does not yet know. BUT, it is coming.

CHAPTER THREE

Finding the Secret on the Battlefield

After Duncan Campbell was saved, at the age of 15, the next four years were years of work and witness. He found himself caught up in attending church meetings, meetings in which the pilgrims of the Faith Mission were holding, and also attending prayer meetings. He found himself going out from the Blackcrofts area to share his testimony of conversion in different places.

As far as we know, the first person Duncan Campbell led to the Lord was his cousin, Archie. He spoke to Archie about his need of Jesus Christ. The words he spoke made a deep impression on Archie. Archie said, "I believed in Duncan. His testimony was sincere. I wished to be like him." That same night Archie went to a house meeting and was saved. [1]

It was during this time that a family moved to the Blackcrofts area that changed Duncan's life forever. Archibald Gray and his wife, Margaret, settled at Blackcrofts with their young family. They had a daughter named, Shona. One night a local Christian took Shona to one of the Pilgrim's meetings. A Mr. Wallace was speaking. At the close of the service, Mr. Wallace asked Shona, "have you given your life to Jesus Christ yet?"

Shona's aunt replied, "She was brought up in a good Christian home."

Shona said, "Oh, but, auntie, I am still not saved."

Mr. Wallace asked Shona, "Wouldn't you like to give your life to Christ?"

Shona replied, "Yes, indeed."

On her knees, in that barn, Shona Gray received Christ. When she stood, she noticed a young lad with red hair standing by the door.

As Duncan Campbell watched Shona leave the barn that night, there was something that flared up in his heart about this new girl who had moved to Blackcrofts. By the next day, he had already made up his mind that one day she would be his wife. [2]

It was during these late teen-age years that some of Duncan's beliefs began to form in his heart. One of those beliefs was the importance of the weekly prayer meeting. Duncan had a difficult time believing that a person's religion was serious if they did not attend the weekly prayer meeting. He came to the conviction that the size of the crowd attending prayer meeting was more important than the size of the crowd on Sunday morning.

It was during these four years that Duncan found himself involved in a deep struggle. The minister and members of the Ardchattan Church where he had been baptized, where his father, Hugh, served as the Precentor had not given their support to the ministry of the Pilgrims of the Faith Mission. He began to wonder why he should continue to attend that church. He found himself faced with a question, "Should he join the other local church where the Rev. D. M. Cameron was the minister?" This church had given so much help and support to the Pilgrims. Duncan talked to his mother about this matter. She said, "Son, if God has lit a lamp in your life, let it shine in the darkness."

Duncan decided to stay in the church of his birth. Years later, the minister of the Ardchattan Church sent for Duncan, asking for his help and prayers, and confessing to Duncan his unfaithfulness , and also sharing with Duncan what it had meant to him for Duncan to stay in the church.

But, suddenly, 1917 came. Gone were the beautiful mountains, lochs and glens of the Scottish Highlands. World War I was raging, and Duncan Campbell, 19 years of age, found himself in the Scottish Army in France. Duncan joined the 51st Division of the Argyll and Sutherland Highlanders. This was an infantry unit posted in the northwest corner of France, fighting one of the most fierce battles of the entire war.

The Flanders Campaign of 1917 was called by David Lloyd George, Prime Minister of England, "Blood and mud! Blood and mud! The campaign of the mud." [3] Duncan's regiment was involved in the Battle for Passchendaele Ridge. The Flanders area is noted for its flatness. Centuries ago the land had been reclaimed from the sea, and the only thing that kept it dry was the careful maintenance of the drainage channels. British, Australian, and Scottish troops fought for Passchendaele Ridge for more than three months. The soldiers lived for months with continuous bombardment. The shelling destroyed the drainage system, and heavy rains that would last for days on end had turned the entire area into an oozing quagmire of yellow mud. The trenches the soldiers tried to dig were filled with slimy, green water. It was indeed a battle of blood and mud. Duncan Campbell was a machine gunner in the Battle for Passchendaele Ridge. In the first assault on the Ridge, 13,000 were killed in a few hours. The slaughter was horrendous. The dead littered the battlefield. Hundreds upon hundreds lay on the battlefield dead, others screamed out in pain, while still others wandered across the battlefield crying, laughing, giggling, or talking to themselves, their minds gone from them.

The life expectancy of a machine-gunner in battle during World War I was thirty minutes, but, God in his mercy, kept watch over Duncan Campbell. On one occasion, Duncan was in the trenches when the Scottish troops watched as clouds of poison gas began to float toward their area. The gas was coming directly toward the 51st Scottish Division. What could these troops do? Could they fix bayonets and charge the gas? Could they get in touch with the artillery and ask them to fire toward the clouds of gas? All of that was folly! There was nothing they could do. Suddenly, a miracle happened. The wind came up and blew the poison gas back toward the German lines. Duncan always felt that God had watched over him in a unique way during the war.

Duncan Campbell's greatest battle during World War I was with himself. He had been cradled in the midst of godliness, sheltered in a godly home, nurtured in family devotions, protected by a praying father and mother, but, now, in the army, he found himself in the midst of extreme ungodliness. He had so many invitations to abandon his faith, to throw away all his principles. Duncan carried with him a picture of Shona Gray, the girl he intended to marry. When he was tempted and invited by other soldiers, he would pull out the photograph of Shona and tell the soldiers he would rather remain faithful to her.

Duncan remembered one occasion when the fighting was so fierce. Soldiers were being cut down all around him. The sound of machine guns, bombs, and the screaming of the wounded increased in his ears. Finally, Duncan cried out, "Oh God, get me out of here and I will serve You with my whole heart." That is a promise he never forgot.

One episode occurred that colored Duncan's conviction concerning death-bed repentance for the rest of his life. One night his outfit was waiting in the trenches. They were going to make a charge the next morning toward the German lines. Seven Scottish soldiers came to Duncan and said, "Duncan, we notice that you pray. Would you pray for us?" He did, and then asked each one of the soldiers to pray for themselves and to ask Christ to save them. They each one prayed and asked Christ to come into their lives. Oh, what prayers they prayed! One of the soldiers prayed, "God, get me out of here, and I will never neglect church again." They were sincere. As these men were praying, lights appeared and the soldiers prepared to leave the trenches. The charge was on. Immediately, four of the men were killed. That night, Duncan sent a messenger to the three who had lived and asked them to come to his trench for a prayer meeting. The messenger arrived just as these soldiers had received their rum ration. They sent word back to Duncan Campbell, "Go back and tell Campbell and his prayer-meeting to go to hell." Duncan Campbell said, "They were no more saved than the devil." Duncan Campbell said, "God is not unwilling to show mercy at the eleventh hour, witness the dying thief; but I fear, in too many cases, there is little genuine desire for mercy."[4]

Duncan Campbell found himself surrounded by debauchery, drunkenness, and gross immorality. He saw what animals men could be. On one occasion a beer barrel had been broken and the contents spilled out into the mud. Rather than lose their ration of beer, the soldiers went down on their hands and knees to drink the beer out of the mud, which was soaked with human blood.

Duncan Campbell was shocked to find there was always a principle of evil working in him. There was a sense that he felt in bondage. Now, he never doubted his salvation. That which happened down in the straw in the barn that night as a 15 year-old was always real to him. But, his mind was bombarded with wrong thoughts, impure thoughts. He seemed to always be fighting an inner conflict. He found there were powers resident in him that were more than a match for him. He had received Christ, been born again, and, he wanted to follow the Savior, but he found another law within him, at war with the life he wanted to live in Christ. He could say with Paul, "I thank God through Jesus Christ our Lord. So then with the mind I myself serve the law of God; but with the flesh the law of sin." (Romans 7:25)

It was during this time that Duncan adopted a verse of Scripture that became his life-long prayer. It was the prayer of David, "Hold up my goings in thy paths, that my footsteps slip not." (Psalms 17:5)

Duncan Campbell's moment of deliverance was about to come. Spring of 1918 came. The military commanders found out that the red-headed machine-gunner had been raised on a farm, and that he should know something about horses. He was transferred from the Infantry to the Cavalry. On April 12, 1918, Duncan Campbell found himself outside Amiens, France engaged in one of the last cavalry charges of the Scottish Army. Campbell in later years said, "I was transferred from the infantry to the cavalry. Oh, God's ways are wonderful. It was because I was transferred to the cavalry that God met with me." [5] The Scottish Cavalry charged across the battlefield, toward the German lines. Withing a few minutes, this new cavalryman, the farm boy from Blackcrofts had his horse shot out from under him. He lay on the ground beside his dead horse, severely wounded, blood flowing freely. Duncan looked out across the battlefield and saw scores of dead horses, other horses wandering riderless through the smoke of the battlefield. When Duncan's horse had fallen, it had rolled over Duncan and injured his spine.

Duncan was firmly convinced in his mind that he was dying. He was bleeding profusely, when, suddenly, a verse of Scripture came to his mind, 'Without holiness, no man shall see the Lord" (Hebrews 12:14). He was deeply conscious that he had been born again, but there was something, just something; he felt so unworthy and very unfit to go out into eternity and meet God. He felt he was going to meet God, and, he had done so little for his Savior. He recalled a hymn that had often been sung at their family devotions, "Must I go and empty-handed, must I meet my Savior so?" It seemed to Duncan that was how he was about to go out and meet his Savior.

Then, a remarkable thing happened! The bugles sounded behind Duncan. The Canadian Cavalry charged across that battlefield where there were hundreds dead and hundreds dying. As the Canadian Cavalry charged by Duncan, one of the horse's hooves struck Duncan Campbell in the spine, and he groaned loudly. That loud groan registered in the mind of that young Canadian Cavalryman. When the battle was over, that young man came back, found Duncan Campbell on the battlefield, leaped from his horse, picked Duncan Campbell up and threw them over the back of his horse. He began galloping toward the Canadian casualty clearing station.

As the horse raced across the battlefield, Duncan, conscious that he was about to die, recalled a prayer he had heard his father pray many times. It was the prayer of Robert Murray MacCheyne, Duncan prayed that prayer, "Lord, make me as holy as a saved sinner can be."

AND, GOD DID IT!!! God swept into Duncan Campbell's life and in the matter of a few moments he had an experience that he did not think possible this side of heaven. The Holy Spirit swept through his life and brought cleansing until, "at that moment I felt as pure as an angel." 6 Duncan thought he was dying, and, in just a moment would be in heaven. But, then, he became conscious of healing. Physically, no! Spiritually, yes!

Throughout the rest of his life, Duncan Campbell referred to this experience in different terms: "baptism of the Holy Ghost", "the fullness of the Holy Spirit", "full salvation." The terms were relatively unimportant to him, it was the practical outcome of the experience that mattered to him. But, Duncan Campbell believed in the baptism of the Holy Spirit after the experience of salvation.

The Canadian Cavalryman brought Duncan to the casualty clearing station. You need to understand that, at this time, Duncan Campbell did not speak English. He only spoke his native language, Gaelic. At the casualty clearing station, he was laid on a cot. He was too weak to sing, too weak to carry on a conversation, too weak from the severe loss of blood. Duncan said all he could do was just keep repeating a verse of one of the Psalms, "Bless the Lord, O my soul: and all that is within me, bless his holy name." (Psalm 103:1)

There was not a single person in that casualty clearing station who understood a word of Gaelic. They were Canadians. But, as Duncan repeated this verse from Psalms, God came in convicting power, and, within an hour seven Canadians were saved. It was Duncan Campbell's first experience with Holy Spirit revival. Before Duncan Campbell was taken from this casualty clearing station, he heard these Canadian men testify to what had happened to them. The reality of God's presence, through the praise of His servant, had so charged the atmosphere with the fear of God that these men were convicted of their sin and were gloriously converted.

This first experience of Holy Ghost revival placed in Duncan Campbell's heart a thirst which never went away, a thirst for real revival, a thirst to see the workings of God in the hearts and lives of men and women.

Duncan Campbell was finally transferred back to a hospital in Perth, Scotland. He was finally released to go home after 13 months in the hospital, but, by his own testimony, Duncan Campbell said those were months of revival. He saw the gracious movings of God in the hospital. He said that he would just speak a word about Jesus, and that would do it, people would be saved.

Through the years of his ministry, Duncan Campbell was always reaching forward, pressing toward the mark of the high calling. He said in one of his sermons, "There are those who say they have arrived. They have got it. There are those who give the impression that there is nothing further than the Baptism of the Holy Ghost and speaking in tongues. I would remind you that there are no limits to the attainment in the divine life. We can press upward and onward. If we had exhausted the possibility of advance, we would be the most miserable creatures alive. Conflict will never cease. New converts are always possible." Campbell closed this message with an illustration. During World War I, when Germany was hard pressing the city of Paris, a French General sent this message to his headquarters, "My flanks are broken, my center is yielding. This to me is a glorious opportunity, and I worked hard for it." He attacked, and this battle was the beginning of what led to victory. [7]

CHAPTER FOUR

The Mid-Argyll-Revival

Duncan Campbell returned home from World War I in May, 1919. After eleven months in the hospital, recuperating from his wounds. He was thrilled to once again be back in the Highlands of Scotland. He could once again sit and gaze across Achnacree Bay, walk the country lanes, enjoy the mountain streams and lochs of his homeland.

His parents were anxious for him to enter the ministry. They wanted him to enroll in Bible College and prepare his life for that of a parish minister. Duncan wrestled with this matter greatly. He had great doubts that he was ready for such an undertaking. He spoke only Gaelic. The Bible Colleges taught in English, and many of the churches held their services using the English language. Duncan was always so deeply proud of his native language. For the rest of his life, he always preferred to use the Gaelic Bible. Sometimes Duncan would refer to Gaelic as the language of heaven. He also wondered why he should spend five to seven years preparing for the ministry when God could send revival in a matter of minutes. Had he not just come out of eleven months of revival on the battlefield, and in the hospital?

With the permission of his parents, Duncan Campbell went out into the villages of Argyllshire and "just talked about Jesus." He did not attempt to preach, did not call himself a preacher. He would visit people, read Scripture to them, pray with them, and give his testimony.

After a few months of traveling about the countryside, Duncan Campbell found himself thinking once again about the Pilgrims of the Faith Mission. They had been so instrumental not only in his conversion, but also the conversions of his Father and Mother. In October, 1919, Duncan entered the Faith Mission.

Duncan packed his clothes and moved to Edinburgh to begin his nine-month course of study at the Faith Mission.

The Faith Mission was started in 1886 by John George Govan, a 25-year-old young man who had been challenged as to what his life was to be. The purpose of the Faith Mission was to evangelize the villages and country districts of Scotland. The new band of missionaries that joined the Faith Mission were called Pilgrims. Working in pairs, the Pilgrims would go to a certain area and conduct "missions" or meetings of three to six weeks. During these missions, the Pilgrims would devote their time to meeting the people in their homes, and at night, evangelistic meetings were conducted, in public halls, churches, schools, barns, tents or homes.

The work of the Faith Mission is interdenominational and the work is itinerant. They do not establish any permanent missions or churches. Those who are saved, or revived are encouraged to be a witness for Christ in their own churches.

So, Duncan Campbell found himself in the classroom, learning what it meant to be a Pilgrim. The study Duncan went through consisted of instruction in the knowledge of God and His Word, the Person and work of the Lord Jesus Christ, the Person and work of the Holy Spirit, prayer life, holiness in every-day living, the art of preaching, personal soul-winning, and work among children. All students also received practical experience in visiting, preaching, personal work, open-air witnessing, and other practical areas of everyday life.

During Duncan Campbell's stay at the Faith Mission College, one event happened that made a deep impression on him. One day, during one of Mr. Govan's lectures, he announced that they would all sing a hymn. They began singing,

Here from the world we turn,
   Jesus to seek;
Here may His loving voice
   Graciously speak!
Jesus our dearest Friend,
   While at Thy feet we bend,
Oh, let Thy smile descend!
   'Tis Thee we seek.

Suddenly a boy from the Highlands stood and said, "Mr. Govan, He is my dearest Friend."

The effect was startling. A tide of desire for God swept across everyone who was present. Everyone fell to their knees and remained in prayer for several hours. [1]

Duncan Campbell remained with the Faith Mission for five years. For five years, he saw revival. He saw that which has come to be known as the Mid-Argyll Revival. Campbell said, "For five years,

I saw the hand of God in revival, and I could trace it back to that experience on the horse's back when God blessed me."[2]

When Campbell finished his course of study at the Faith Mission, the students were called together for the announcement of mission locations. When Mr. Govan announced that Duncan Campbell would be going to the North Irish District, Duncan was deeply disappointed. He had wanted to return to his beloved Highlands to spread the gospel.

I can well understand Duncan Campbell's love for the Highlands of Scotland. On my trip to that region, I fell in love with the country and the people. I have never visited a more beautiful area with the majestic mountains, waterfalls streaming down, the lochs tucked into every valley, the lush, green scenery in every direction.

But, being an obedient Pilgrim, Duncan Campbell and his young Irish pardner went to Antrim County, Ireland in 1920. An old Highland revivalist, Rev. D. T. Mackay, of the Isle of Tiree once said, "If ye canna rouse the Lord's people, rouse the devil."[3] These two young Pilgrims did both in Ireland. They saw lives changed, people saved. They labored for six weeks in this mission. At the close of the mission, a letter arrived from the Faith Mission asking Duncan to return to Scotland, and begin to labor in Argyllshire. For the next five years, Duncan worked in Argyllshire and parts of Inverness-shire.

Duncan's preaching was bold and straight-forward. He seemed to speak to people with eternity in his heart. One woman told Duncan that she didn't need to hear him preach, that she had been through the Bible herself. Duncan replied, "Perhaps so, Madam, but have you allowed the Bible to go through you?" On another occasion, a young man was mocking Duncan as he spoke. Duncan finally turned to the young man and said, "Young man, your head won't be so high, and your speech won't be so bold when the waves of death are lapping the shores of your body."[4]

Duncan's first assignment after returning from Ireland was the Island of Mull. There were many victories and much opposition on this isle. On one occasion, a young woman came into the meeting, seemingly in great distress. Duncan took his Bible, went to the young lady to counsel her. Duncan's fellow Pilgrim stopped him, and said, "Wait! I'll speak to her." The young Pilgrim went to the young lady and said, "Get out of here, you child of the devil." With a scream the young woman ran from the church. It was later found out that she had been planted in the meeting in order to bring disturbance. [5]

Duncan and his fellow-pilgrim went from the Isle of Mull on to many other places where God sent revival. They preached on the Isle of Iona, where the first Christian missionaries to Scotland had arrived; to Morven, with its beautiful mountains; to Ballachulish; to Kinlochleven.

Finally, Duncan and his pardner went to the Island of Skye in 1924. They received a cold reception. Only a few attended the meetings. There was even much open antagonism. Duncan gave himself to prayer. He found himself walking the country roads at night praying for revival. In the village were three young women who knew how to pray. They went home to pray. Duncan went to a barn to pray. After midnight, one of the young women ran to the home of another young woman crying out, "God has come! God has come! He is going to work. But we must pray right through." They continued to pray until six in the morning.

The next night, the fire of God fell on the meeting. There was great conviction of sin. Attendance began to grow in the meeting. The awesome presence of God was felt all over the community.

One of those who was converted at this meeting on the Island of Skye was a man named Neilag. He was a drinker, and known as very wild. Some people were passing a petition to get Duncan Campbell out of the village. Since Neilag was one of the prominent men of the village, they secured his services. He went to the meeting to get some signatures, and was saved.

Neilag witnessed everywhere. He spoke to everyone he met about Jesus Christ. People would be walking down the street and see Neilag and another person on their knees in prayer.

But, one night a man came to the church and said, "Mr. Campbell, Neilag has gone back. I saw him going to the lodge with a bottle in his pocket." Neilag had been invited to a dinner in honor of his grandmother's birthday, and it was the custom for each guest to bring a bottle of whiskey.

But, Neilag later told his story. He arrived at the birthday celebration. His friends were delighted to see him, thinking he had turned his back on his new faith. To prove they were not pagans, they asked him to say the prayer before they ate. Neilag prayed for about twenty minutes, asking God to save them. Then, Neilag took the bottle from his pocket, poured the contents into glasses, and, then, he told the church people, "I made them drink the toast to my grandmother with the milk from the brown cow!"[6]

But, a low point in Duncan Campbell's life occurred on the Isle of Skye. He suddenly became very ill. He was confined to bed. He had an examination by a doctor, and he suspected tuberculosis. The people of the local church began taking care of Duncan. They would take turns sitting by his bedside, day and night. These people could not understand why there should be this setback in the revival.

But, one young woman, who had prayed so much for the revival, was not daunted. She knew that God had promised to bless the meetings. She knew that God would not fail to keep His Word.

When her turn came to sit by Duncan's bedside, she knelt to pray beside the bed, "Lord, we invited him here, now it looks like we have him on our hands. But Lord, You are going to heal him and when You do, look after him, for the dear man hasn't the sense to look after himself."

From the moment the young lady finished her prayer, a change came over Duncan. The following night he was back in the pulpit, preaching with all of the passion he had in the past.

Duncan had been with the Faith Mission for five years. Unsettling questions began to loom in his mind. These questions brought about the lowest period in Duncan's life. He is about to enter the time of walking away from the fullness of the Holy Spirit.

CHAPTER   FIVE

Years of Barren Wilderness

Duncan Campbell spent five years as a Pilgrim with the Faith Mission. But, during the year of 1924, questions began to rise in his mind. There were questions about his health. Was he healthy enough to continue the long hours and rapid pace of a Pilgrim's life? There was the question of his status with the Faith Mission. If his health failed him, what would that do to his position as a Pilgrim? And, then, there were the question of his love for Shona. He had hopes of marriage, but so many things troubled him about that.

It had been eleven years since he had stood against a wall in a meeting house and had seen Shona across the room, deciding that night that this was the girl he would marry, eleven long years since that night when he had watched her give her life to Christ.

When Duncan Campbell left the army in 1919, Shona was enrolled in the Bible Training Institute in Glasgow. She had committed herself to the Algiers Mission Board. Duncan had proposed to her at that time, but, not wishing to go to the mission field engaged, Shona declined the proposal.

Two years later, Shona came home. She and Duncan met at a Keswick Convention. On the train journey home, they had the opportunity to sit down and discuss the future. On the train, they looked for a place where they could talk in private. They found the guard's room. He gave them permission to use it. In that room, the only seats available were sacks of cabbage. Sitting on the sacks of cabbage, Duncan proposed marriage to Shona, and she accepted. From that moment on, Duncan said that he always had a weakness for cabbage.

In July, 1925, Duncan wrote a letter to Mr. Govan tendering his resignation from the Faith Mission. In December, 1925 , Duncan and Shona were married in the Prince of Wales Hall in Glasgow. They spent their honeymoon on the Isle of Skye, in the town of Dunvegan.

From the time of his resignation until the wedding, Duncan had been a farm laborer. While on his honeymoon, he was invited to preach in the United Free Church. Because of that sermon, he was asked to stay on the Isle of Skye as a missionary.

On the southern end of the Isle of Skye is the tiny, remote village of Ardvasar. The little church at Ardvasar, sitting beside the road, had no minister. The Presbytery of Skye asked Duncan to become minister of this little church.

The southern end of Skye is known as "the garden of Skye." Trees abound. Lush foliage is everywhere. Fern grows thick under every tree. Heather fills the hillsides.

On my trip to the Isle of Skye, I drove into the village of Ardvasar, stopped at the hotel and asked where the church might be. The young lady said there was no church in Ardvasar. I was driving up the road, saw a dear elderly lady walking her dog. I got out of the car and asked about the old church in Ardvasar. She said, "Yes, it is just across the street from the hotel, but it is no longer a church. It is now a home." She advised me to go to an apartment about one block down the road. She said there was an old retired minister who lived there. He could tell me what I needed to know.

I knocked on the door of that apartment, and came into contact with one of the kindest, most sweet-spirited men I have ever met, Donald Angie Maclean. Mr. Maclean had been a missionary on the Isle of Skye for thirty-three years. He knew Duncan Campbell quite well. We both laughed as he told me one of Duncan Campbell's quotes. Mr. Maclean said he had heard Duncan Campbell say this many, many times. As people would make excuses about not coming to church; have to take care of the farm, have to take care of their livestock. Duncan Campbell, in his sermon, would say, "Your old, brown cow won't take you to heaven."

Mr. Maclean went with me and my wife down the street to the old church. Sitting on the south side of the street, white, majestic, still looking like a church, was a building wrapped in hedges. Across the street was the manse (parsonage) where Duncan Campbell and his new bride lived. The church sits on a promontory, with the manse on the north side, and the pounding sea on the south side.
The church building is surrounded by a rock wall. On the street side of that wall is imbedded a concrete square with these words, "The Old Church."

When Duncan was minister of the church at Ardvasar, there were three denominations in the small village; the Church of Scotland, the Free Church, and the United Free Church. It was during his time as minister of this church that negotiations began to attempt to reunite the United Free Church and the Church of Scotland. Those who were opposed to reuniting were afraid that they might be returning to the old system of patronage.

The split in the two groups had occurred in 1843 in what has come to be called,. "The Disruption of 1843." During that time, the Church of Scotland was supported by state endowments instead of voluntary contributions. Patronage was the appointment of the ministers by wealthy land- owners rather than their selection by the people of the church.

Duncan Campbell sided with those who were opposed to the merger. He believed that the evangelical message would have more freedom and power if the United Free Church remained separate. In 1929, the merger was completed. The Presbyteries of the Isle of Skye were very much in favor of the merger. So, when the merger occurred, Duncan Campbell resigned the pulpit in the village of Ardvasar.

As I drove away from Ardvasar that day, my mind was on a young man, age 27, who came to this wild, windy, beautiful land, to preach the gospel of Jesus Christ. It was his first pastorate. He preached with fervor, visited his people diligently, but, still, felt he had to leave the church because of the merger between two denominations.

The battle over the merger of the Church of Scotland and the United Free Church was raging all over Scotland. Many were in favor of the merger, others bitterly opposed.

On the north-east coast of Scotland is the small, fishing town of Balintore. The entire church family of Balintore voted to break their association with the neighboring church of Nigg and remain United Free. The United Free Church of Balintore was formed, and, in March, 1930, Duncan Campbell was appointed as minister of this church. It was here that Duncan was formally ordained and now could administer the sacraments.

Duncan was always a forthright, uncompromising preacher. He never "played to the gallery." When he started preaching at Balintore, he talked to them honestly and straight-forward. He told the older unconverted people they were "gathering speed for hell." He warned the youth to place no hope in the ghost of future repentance. He said, "Be careful, lest God should refuse the devil's leavings." [1]

The church at Balintore was a new congregation. They had no

church building. They met in a little meeting house that was too small. Often, because of space, communion was held under the starry skies in a nearby field.

Balintore was a fishing village. Money was scarce, but a new church building was opened on December 7, 1932. A manse (parsonage) was built right beside the church.

In 1922, revival had swept through the village of Balintore. In that year two Faith Mission Pilgrims had preached in this village, and now, most of the members of Duncan's church were converts of that revival

Duncan had many blessings and many sorrows while serving as minister in Balintore. In 1939, a twenty-one year old, Spirit-filled young lady, Kate, suddenly took ill and died. On October 15, 1939 five of Balintore's young people died when the battleship, "Royal Oak", was torpedoed by a German U-boat in a harbor at the Orkney Islands.

Five months later, March, 1940, after having served for ten years as minister, Duncan Campbell resigned the church at Balintore. The people were shocked. They had shared joys and sorrows, laughter and tears. In his last sermon to them, Duncan Campbell said, "Will all these years be in vain, the talks, the fellowship, the warnings, the entreaties? O, sinner, come! Yet there is room." [2]

Duncan spent ten fruitful years at Balintore. Church membership had increased. A new church building and new manse had been erected. Duncan and Shona's own family had increased to three boys and two girls; Sheena, Margaret, Ewan, Archie, and John When the Campbell family left town, the entire congregation gathered at the train station to see them off.

Duncan had accepted the pastorate of the United Free Church in Falkirk, Scotland. But, something had happened to Duncan. Did it occur at Falkirk, or Balintore, or Ardvasar? Or, did it occur at all three places, gradually? Let Duncan describe it himself, "I came under the influence of professors that did not believe in the authority nor inspiration of the Word of God. I found myself doubting the first three chapters of Genesis. Now, it's true that I was evangelical in my preaching. I was called on to preach in special missions. I was a popular Keswick Convention speaker, because I was Campbell of the

Argyll Revival, but I was moving in a barren wilderness." 3

Falkirk was an industrial town. There was much more material prosperity than the village of Balintore had known. Duncan saw there was a state of spiritual indifference. He preached the same sermons, but not the same results. He preached with the same fervor, but was not seeing anything happen.

This could have been a combination of two things. It well might have been that the town of Falkirk was spiritually indifferent. But, the difficulty might have been in Duncan's own spirit. While I was in the city of Falkirk, the Free Church minister told me that he had read a statement that Duncan Campbell had made. The statement was to the effect that Falkirk was the most difficult place he served as minister. While I was there, an older man said, "Yes, it was difficult, but, probably because Duncan was away from God."

When I arrived in Falkirk, I had a most difficult time locating the church where Duncan Campbell served as minister. First, I went downtown where there are two magnificent church buildings, side by side. I entered the "Falkirk Old and St. Modan's Parish Church." This is the oldest church in central Scotland. The present building dates from 1811. In fact, the city received its name from the ancient church which stood here more than 1200 years ago. The church received the name many centuries ago of, "Faw-kirk", "the speckled church."

In the office of this old church, a lady was most kind to help me. She called several older members of the congregation, but no one was familiar with Duncan Campbell, or his ministry in this city. Finally, she called the Free Church minister in the city. He told me that the church where Duncan Campbell served was no longer in existence, but the church building was now the chapel of the Collumbine Funeral Home. My wife and I traveled to the funeral home and got acquainted with Sid Collumbine, the owner. He was a most gracious man, extremely helpful. When he bought the church building, he had the outside of the building remodeled, but, he said the inside was exactly as it was when Duncan Campbell was minister. An interesting note: The pulpit in the church was made from the headboard of a bed.

I asked Sid Collumbine if he knew where the manse (parsonage) was located. He did not, but, he said there was an old man who had been a member of this church, who would know. Mr. Collumbine showed us where the old man lived. And, I had the privilege of meeting Charles and Mary Ramsey, a most gracious couple.

As we sat down in their living room, Charles and Mary Ramsey related that Duncan Campbell had married them in 1941 while he was minister at Falkirk. They told me many interesting and wonderful stories about Campbell. He was a forceful preacher, a delight to be around. They laughed about his forgetfulness. One time, when he was minister in Falkirk, he was out in the field, working. He was dressed in old work clothes. Suddenly, he remembered he was supposed to be somewhere   preaching. He hurriedly left, made the meeting, preaching in his old work clothes. Campbell was a very forceful preacher. On one occasion he struck the pulpit, and broke a bone in his hand. He would stomp his feet often to emphasize a point.

I asked Charles and Mary Ramsey if they knew where the manse was located. Charles said, "Oh, yes, on Gibsongray Street. Mary and I got married in the manse." We drove to the manse, stood in the street and looked at it. I was particularly interested in seeing the upstairs room of the manse, for it was here that Duncan Campbell had a great experience with the Lord, when he came back to a fullness of the Holy Spirit. That experience changed his life.

As a church minister in Falkirk, Campbell was extremely busy. He spent hours in study. He prayed and prayed. He traveled miles each week on his motorbike to visit his people. On Sunday, he preached four services; three in the church and one, an open-air service. He preached a monthly Gaelic service, plus having many other preaching engagements in Scotland and Ireland.

One highlight of the ministry of Duncan Campbell in Falkirk involved a young man who had come home from the army. He was a heavy drinker and found himself in church one Sunday morning. At the close of the service, Duncan Campbell performed a baptismal service of a little baby. This young man sat on the back row of the church. Suddenly, he was gripped by God. He saw the piety and innocence of the baby being baptized, and the evil of his own life. He got up and left the church. Campbell saw him leave, turned the service over to an Elder, and began to chase this young man down the street. He asked what was wrong. The young man told him. They walked down the street to the manse. Duncan Campbell shared with him the story of the Prodigal Son, and then asked the young man, "Are you willing to be a fool for Christ's sake?" The young man said that he was. They knelt to pray, and a clear, unmistakable change came into his life. The young man said, "I got down on my knees one man, and rose up another." This young man went on to a life as a gospel minister, and has recently retired. 4

But, Duncan had lost something! The experience he had on horseback in France was receding into the background. The reality of Christ was becoming dim to him. Much of the time he felt frustration and felt that he was a failure. Duncan Campbell said, "For all these years my altar was broken. For all these years, I moved in a barren wilderness. It is true that I was evangelical in my preaching, I visited my people. On several occasions I was asked to conduct special missions, and I was a popular Keswick Convention speaker, but, knowing in my heart that I was not right with God. Oh, what an experience!" 5

This was the lowest point of Duncan Campbell's life in the ministry. He was holding on to past experiences, and trying to build a reputation centered upon those past experiences.

During this time, he began to honestly search his own life. He talked to his wife about it. She could hear him praying at night, "Lord, tell me what I should do."

A return to the old life of revival is about to come to Duncan Campbell. His life is about to change, for God is always at work in the shadows.

CHAPTER SIX

God at Work in the Shadows

Duncan Campbell had known the fullness of the Lord. He never forgot the day, in 1918, on the horse's back in France, when God filled him with the Holy Spirit. It was that short prayer, "Oh God, make me as holy as a saved sinner can be." And God did it! He had lived in that fullness for several years. He served five years as a Pilgrim with the Faith Mission, seeing revival in Ireland and in the Highlands of Scotland. But, then came twenty-four years serving as a church Minister. Somewhere during those years as Minister, Duncan lost that fullness of the Holy Spirit that he so treasured. Feeling himself a failure, Duncan was crying out to God, asking Him what he should do. For Duncan, prayer had become a burden, and the Word of God, a dead Word.

Oh, but God is always working in the shadows! God's ways are always mysterious and hidden. When Moses asked to see the glory of God, God said to him, "I will make all my goodness pass before you, and I will proclaim the name of the Lord before you; and will be gracious to whom I will be gracious, and will show mercy on whom I will show mercy. You can not see my face: for there shall no man see me, and live. Behold, there is a place by me, and you shall stand upon a rock, and it shall come to pass, while my glory passes by, that I will put you in a cleft of the rock, and will cover you with my hand while I pass by: And I will take away my hand, and you shall see my back; but my face shall not be seen." (Exodus 33:19-23)

The ways of God are always so strange. They are not man's ways. We almost never see God coming, we only see Him going. God moves by us, and we experience His glory, then, as He passes by, we see His back and say, "That was God working in the shadows." We must live life forward, but we only understand life backward.

God was working in the shadows to bring Duncan Campbell back to His glory. And, when God does a work, He always does it right.

On November 15, 1947, God came out of the shadows and passed by Duncan Campbell in all of His glory.

Duncan was sitting in his upstairs study in the manse, preparing a message he was to preach at the Keswick Convention in Edinburgh. It was 5:00 in the morning. He heard singing coming from the parlor downstairs. He sat back in his chair and listened. There was something haunting about the song, and about the singer. It was his sixteen-year-old daughter, Sheena, singing in the parlor. Sheena was already a mission volunteer. She had surrendered her life to go to the nation of Nepal as a missionary.

Duncan made his way downstairs, slipped into the parlor, and sat down. He just listened while Sheena finished singing the song. She was singing:

Coming, coming, yes, they are,
Coming, coming from afar;
From the Indies and the Gandes,
Steady flows that living stream,
To love's ocean, to His fulness,
Calvary, their wondering theme.

As Sheena sang, something stirred in Duncan's heart. When she finished singing, she came over, sat down on her father's lap, and said, "Daddy, I would like to talk to you."

Duncan replied, "Sheena, I would be happy to talk to you, but, first, what is it that is moving you this morning?"

Sheena replied, "Oh, Daddy, Isn't Jesus wonderful? Isn't Jesus wonderful?"

Duncan asked her, "Sheena, what is it that makes Jesus so wonderful to you at 5:00 in the morning?"

Sheena said, "Daddy, I have just spent an hour with Jesus, and He is so wonderful." [1] Then, she said, "Daddy, for several days I have been battling against asking you a question, but I must do it. Daddy, when you were a young Pilgrim with the Faith Mission, you saw revival. Daddy, why is it not with you now, as it once was? Daddy, how is it that you are not seeing revival now?" Then, Sheena hit Duncan with a crushing question, "Daddy, you have a large congregation and many are joining the church, but, when did you last kneel beside a poor sinner and lead him to Jesus?"

That question shook Duncan Campbell deep in his soul. He went on to the Keswick Convention, where he was to preach. The two keynote addresses were to be Duncan Campbell and Dr. Tom Fitch from Belfast, Ireland. Duncan preached his sermon, and, later said how glad he was when that was over. [2]

When it came time for Dr. Fitch to preach, he announced that he was departing from his prepared message, and just wanted to give his testimony. That testimony shook Duncan Campbell to the core. Duncan became very conscious that he was not fit to be sitting on that platform. The pride in his own heart was revealed. He was sitting there to speak at a Keswick Convention, full of pride that he was to preach at five of these conventions during that year. On the way home Dr. Fitch's message kept stirring his soul. And, that question of his daughter's kept ringing in his ear, "Daddy, when did you last lead a soul to Jesus?"

On the way home, Duncan resolved in his heart that, unless God did something in his heart, unless God gave him back what he had lost, that he would resign from the ministry and go into business.

When Duncan reached home, he told his wife he would eat no supper. He told his wife, Shona, and his daughter, Sheena, that he was going upstairs to his study and seek a meeting with God. He said, "I will not come out to eat or to drink until I am right with God."

He placed a rug in front of the fire, and lay down on the rug. He was beginning his search for what he had lost. He began to cry out to God to forgive him. He found himself doing battle with the powers of darkness. Duncan felt that the devil was whispering to him that God no longer had any use for him. Suddenly, a verse of Scripture came to his mind, "For the Lord will not cast off his people, neither will He forsake his inheritance." (Psalms 94:14) This verse was followed by another. It was the Scripture that he had quoted in the Canadian casualty clearing station when he had been filled with the Holy Spirit on the battlefield in France, "Bless the Lord, O, my soul: and all that is within me, bless His holy name. Who forgives all your iniquities; who heals all your diseases." (Psalms 103:1,3)

At that moment, Duncan Campbell knew that God had come to meet with him. He had come, not only to meet with Duncan, but to bring him back to that glorious experience in the fullness of the blessing of the Holy Spirit. Duncan said as he lay there on that rug, he could feel this power coming over him. [3] In later years, Duncan could never describe this adequately. Wave after wave of love flooding over him. God spoke to Duncan the word of forgiveness, the word of pardon and the word of recommission.

But, when Duncan realized a calling to go back into the work of evangelism, there seemed to be a fading of his joy, for Duncan had an unwillingness in his heart to do this. He found himself asking questions, "How would he support his family?" His wife had promised Sheena a new coat for her birthday. This would be impossible if he had no salary. The glory seemed to fade in that upstairs study.

It was now 2:00 in the morning, suddenly, the door of the study opened and Sheena came in. That dear, young daughter lay down on the rug next to her Daddy and prayed, "O, Jesus, keep his reason to Daddy." She was afraid that her daddy was losing his mind. Duncan said he had never felt more sane in his life. Then, Sheena said, "Daddy, whatever it costs, go through with God."

Then, Sheena said a most remarkable thing, "Daddy, I believe you are fighting the question if you should go back to the Faith Mission, because I am fully persuaded that God is asking you to go back."

Then, Sheena spoke the words that sounded to Duncan as the voice of God Himself, "Daddy, perhaps you are wondering how you can look after us. I know that you promised to buy me a new coat for my birthday, but, Daddy, Mother will be quite willing to fix my old coat. You needn't buy me a new coat." Here was a young lady who was as anxious to be well-dressed as any young person, but more than willing to have her old coat fixed so that she could make it easier for her daddy to do the will of God.

In that moment, Duncan said, "Yes" to God. Flood tides of glory came over him again and again. Duncan said he immediately seemed to be in a trance gazing into the caverns of death. He saw the agonies of hell. With horror he saw thousands from the Highlands and the Western Islands drifting into hell. He heard a voice calling to him, "Go to them, go to them!" 4

An interesting aside to this story happened a short time later. Duncan was preaching in a certain town, and revival came. One of the leading merchants came to Duncan and asked him how many family members he had. Duncan told him. The merchant said, "You know that practically all the weavers in my plant were saved during this revival. I feel that I should give you a peace offering of thankfulness. I want you to come to my office tomorrow and I will give you some

Harris Tweed. You take the tweed home. You get yourself, your wife and each of your children to select two lengths of tweed, one for a suit and one for a coat for the men; and your wife and daughters enough for a dress and a coat" 5 That is how God works. Duncan Campbell did the will of God, and Sheena got her new coat.

For the rest of his life, Duncan Campbell never got away from the vision God gave him of hell in his study that night. He really believed that souls were lost without God. He felt he had to warn people of God's way of escape through Jesus Christ. That night a certain peace settled over his heart, and he realized that God would see that he take up the ministry he had left years before. Campbell knew that, in a moment, God had restored all the years the locust had devoured. He came out of his study with two certain convictions: Christ's willingness to save the 'whosoever', and the awful state of those lost in hell.

Throughout his ministry, one of the ringing cries in Duncan's preaching was the fact that God can always restore, that God can always reclaim. He believed deeply that the blood of Jesus Christ can reach deeper than the stain of sin can go. Duncan Campbell often used an illustration from the life of Dr. Stuart Holman. There was a businessman, a member of Dr. Holman's church, who was mightily used of God. In an unguarded hour, the businessman did something that placed him in prison for seven years. Dr. Holman would often visit this businessman. One day this man discovered the cleansing power of the blood of Jesus, a God who would forgive. He wrote a verse and requested that it be added to that unscriptural hymn-poem that some people sing, "the bird with the broken pinion never soars as high again." The businessman wrote this verse:

The soul that comes to Jesus,
Through failure, shame or pain
By His wondrous love and mercy
Will soar as high again.

On Sunday morning following this great experience of renewal, Duncan Campbell stepped into his pulpit at the church in Falkirk and apologized to the church for not being what he claimed to be. He related what had happened to him in his study. The following day, Monday, five of his elders resigned and left the church. One Elder remarked that he would not have a fool in the pulpit.

Duncan wrote three letters of resignation; one to the Session Clerk, another to the Presbytery Convener, and another to the Clerk of Assembly. In these letters, he said he wished to remain a member of the Presbytery and denomination, and he wanted to retain his status as a minister. Now, Duncan Campbell is free, free to go out, free to claim the glory of God, and he is deliriously happy in the Holy Spirit.

Duncan approached the Faith Mission about the possibility of returning to the Faith Mission as an evangelist. The Mission was, at first, reluctant to consider Duncan because of his age, and the size of his family. Duncan Campbell was now fifty years of age, and had five children. Traditionally, the Faith Mission had accepted young, single men and women to go out and do the work of the Mission.

In October, 1948, Duncan Campbell was selected to serve with the Faith Mission, doing the work of an evangelist, in the Highlands of Scotland. He began this work on January 1, 1949. Campbell found that his old sense of failure was gone. A new spirit was now in him, a spirit of confidence, a spirit of glory. There was now an awareness of the reality of Jesus Christ in his personal life, and in his preaching.

Campbell's first journey in this new fullness of the Holy Spirit was to the Isle of Skye. He was returning to the scene of past experiences. He had served on Skye over twenty-five years earlier as a worker with the Faith Mission, and also as minister of the church at Ardvasar. Now, he is coming back to Skye with a new vision and a new spirit.

Campbell ministered for almost one full year on Skye. He saw things that he had longed to see for over a quarter of a century. He saw revival on the Isle of Skye.

BUT, God is still at work in the shadows. When God is doing His work, He not only works with one person. He will do His work in every area, so that His will can be performed.

While God was bringing Duncan Campbell back to Himself in the town of Falkirk, God was also working in the hearts and lives of some people on the Isle of Lewis in the Hebrides Islands.

The Isle of Lewis was no stranger to revival. This isle had a history of darkness and slumber for many, many years. For centuries the people of Lewis had been bound with superstitions and paganism.

For centuries there was no Gaelic Bible. In fact, the authorities of Scotland believed that the Gaelic language had to be rooted out. It was forbidden to teach the Gaelic language. However, there came a change in policy and the New Testament was translated into Gaelic in 1767, then the complete Bible was available in 1801.

The first great revival to come to the Isle of Lewis was in 1828, under the preaching of Alexander Macleod. Mrs. Steward Mackenzie of Seaforth had great sympathy for evangelical preaching. She was responsible for bringing Alexander Macleod to the Isle of Lewis. He was admitted as minister of the church at Uig in 1824. He began preaching. Soon large crowds were making their way to Uig to hear him preach. It was not long until they had to move out of the church building and meet in the open-air because of the size of the crowds. In 1828 the fire of God fell on this church and revival came to Lewis.

Revival also came to the Isle of Lewis in 1939. This revival was short-lived because of the outbreak of World War II. Young men and women went off to the war, and the revival subsided when they left.

While I was visiting the Isle of Lewis, I was in the home of Alexander and Mary Murray, who live in the town of Stornoway. Mary Murray was saved during the revival of 1939. She lived in the village of Shader. Mary was raised in a Christian home. She went to church. She mentioned a godly man, Roderick Martin, who lived next door to her family. He had a great influence on Mary's life. When revival came, Mary told about the "after-meetings" that would be held in the home of John Smith, a blacksmith in Shader. She said as they would walk from the church to the home of John Smith, she would get behind John Smith and listen to him talk about the church service.

Mary said there were nineteen new converts at the Carloway church on the Sunday World War II broke out. She said the cloth on the pews was wet with tears on that Sunday. People were weeping, not only from joy at the ones who had been saved, but also from sadness for the young people who would be going off to war.

Mary Murray went off to the war, serving as a nurse. She came back to visit during the great revival of 1949-53. She heard Duncan Campbell preach at the Barvas Church several times. Mary said he was a wonderful preacher.

But, now, it is 1949. Duncan Campbell has been filled with the Holy Spirit, and is preaching on the Isle of Skye. Now, God begins to work in the hearts of two elderly women and seven men in the village of Barvas.

The churches of Lewis had become deeply concerned about the spiritual state of the churches. Especially they were alarmed at the lack of young people who attended church. There was not one single young person who attended church at Barvas, and only a few at the other churches. In High School, the pupils were speaking of conversion as 'the plague", something from which to keep away at all costs. 6

The Free Church Presbytery of Lewis met, and drafted the following declaration. This declaration was to be read from every pulpit on the Isle of Lewis:

"The Presbytery of Lewis, having taken into consideration the low state of vital religion within their own bounds, and throughout the land generally, call upon their faithful people in all their congregations to take a serious view of the present dispensation of divine displeasure manifested, not only in the chaotic conditions of international politics and morality, but also, and especially, in the lack of spiritual power from gospel ordinances, and to realize that these things plainly indicated that the Most High has a controversy with the nation. They note especially the growing carelessness toward Sabbath observance and public worship, the light regard of solemn vows and obligations so that the sacraments of the church-especially that of baptism-tend to become in too many cases an offence to God rather than a means of grace to the recipients, and the spreading abroad of the spirit of pleasure which has taken such a hold of the younger generation that all regard for anything higher appears with very few exceptions to have been utterly dismissed from their thoughts.

'The Presbytery affectionately plead with their people, especially with the youth of the church, to take these matters to heart and to make serious inquiry as to what must be the end, should there be no repentance; and they call upon every individual as before God to examine his or her life in the light of that responsibility which pertains to us all, that haply, in the divine mercy, we may be visited with the spirit of repentance and may turn again unto the Lord whom we have so grieved with our iniquities and waywardness. Especially would they warn their young people of the devil's man-traps- the cinema and the public-houses.' [7]

The minister of the church at Barvas., at this time, was Rev. James Murray Mackay. He read this declaration to his congregation on a Sunday. During the next week he took the declaration to the home of two elderly sisters who were not able to attend church. He read this declaration to the two sisters, Peggy and Christine Smith. Peggy was 84 years of age and blind. Christine was 82 years of age and suffered with severe arthritis. The Smith sisters lived south of the church, next door to the police station in Barvas.

God is at work in the shadows! When the minister read this declaration to the Smith sisters, they committed themselves to prayer about this matter. They spoke only Gaelic, so their prayers went before the Lord in their native language. In prayer, God gave to Peggy Smith a vision. She saw the church of her father (the Barvas Church) filled with people, packed with young people. There came to both of these sisters the promise of God, "I will pour water upon him that is thirsty, and floods upon the dry ground." (Isaiah 44:3)

The sisters sent for their minister, Rev. James Murray Mackay. Peggy told him of her vision. The minister asked, "What do you think we ought to do?"

Peggy replied, "What? Give yourselves to prayer! Give yourselves to waiting on God! Get your elders together, your deacons together, and spend at least two night a week waiting on God in prayer. If you will do that at the other end of the parish, my sister and I will get down on our knees here in our home from 10:00 at night until 2:00 or 3:00 in the morning." [8]

Rev. Mackay called his elders and deacons together and shared with them the vision of Peggy Smith. Three of the men who met with the minister to pray were Kenneth Macdonald, John Smith, and Roderick Macleod. For months, this minister and six of his men met in a small barn on the north side of the parish. Peggy and Christine Smith met in their home on the south side of the parish. They prayed. They waited on God, praying two nights a week from 10:00 until 2:00 or 3:00 in the morning. This continued for three months. Nothing happened!

But, one night, while waiting on God in the little barn, one of the deacons, Kenneth Macdonald, rose to his feet, opened his Bible and read part of Psalm 24, "Who shall ascend to the hill of God? Who shall stand in His holy place? He that has clean hands and a pure heart, who has not lifted up his soul unto vanity, nor sworn deceitfully, he shall receive the blessing of the Lord."

This deacon then closed his Bible and addressed his minister and the other elders and deacons in the barn, "It seems to me just so much humbug to be waiting as we are waiting, and praying as we are praying, if we ourselves are not rightly related to God." Then, he lifted both hands toward the heaven, and cried out, "O God, are my hands clean, is my heart pure?" Then Deacon Macdonald fell on his knees in the straw, and in a moment he fell into a trance, unconscious. [9] Suddenly, the FIRE OF GOD FELL in that little barn.

God, who brought a preacher back to Himself in an upstairs study in Falkirk, Scotland; who spoke to two old, infirm sisters; this God is now moving out of the shadows to do His work. The glory of God is about to fall on the Isle of Lewis.

CHAPTER SEVEN

Glory Comes to the Isle of Lewis

When I flew into the airport at Stornoway on the Isle of Lewis on October 2, 2001, I felt that I had landed on holy ground. All the reading I had done, all the listening to tapes, all the praying I had gone through, seemed to come to fruition as I gazed out the airplane window at the green landscape of the Isle of Lewis. Looking across the treeless moorland and meadows of Lewis, I could envision the days of a half century ago when God came down on this small island in all of His glory.

I don't use that word, glory, loosely. The word, glory, in the Old Testament, carries with it the idea of something heavy, something weighty, something of substance. That is what happened on the Isle of Lewis. God came, in all of His glory, and brought something of substance to the people of this island.

Revival was nothing new to the Isle of Lewis. There had been other, great movements of God back across the years. The first revival that came to Lewis was over 200 years ago. The minister in that revival had been led to Christ by a blind evangelist. This minister was called to a large congregation of over 3,000 people. At his first communion, the building could not hold all the people. They met on a hillside. The minister looked out across the vast congregation and said, "I see you are sure for hell." That was the statement God used to bring revival to Lewis. 6 Since that time, the Isle of Lewis had experienced many, different revivals, usually about every thirty to forty years.

It is difficult for me to use the word, revival. In our nation of America, we have used that word to denote a series of meetings where we have preaching and singing. "We are going to have a revival meeting." Unfortunately, most of the time, no revival comes. Duncan Campbell marked a vast difference in evangelism and revival. He said that in evangelism you will have the two, the ten, maybe even the hundreds making profession of faith in Jesus Christ. At the end of the year, you are thankful if half of them are standing, but the community remains untouched. But, in revival, when God really comes, when the winds of heaven really blow, suddenly the whole community becomes God- conscious. 1

Duncan Campbell had the privilege of seeing genuine, authentic revival come to the Isle of Lewis. He said, "Revival begins in an awareness of God gripping a community." [2] It is a time when God steps down and his presence fills the whole community. And, perhaps, in a matter of a few hours, scores or hundreds of people are swept into the kingdom of God. And, they may be saved before they come near a church, or place of worship. Duncan Campbell said that 75% of those saved during the Lewis Revival were saved before listening to a sermon or attending a place of worship. [3] Why? Because God was everywhere. People out tending their livestock would fall under the convicting power of the Holy Spirit. Men sitting at their looms, weaving yarn, would suddenly be gripped by God. Shopkeepers tending their stores would be gripped by Almighty God. Students attending school would suddenly be faced with their sin, and cry out to God. Duncan Campbell said, "Revival is a going of God among His people, and an awareness of God laying hold of the community." [4]

Most people in America today, when they use the word, revival, are speaking of a crusade, a campaign, special meetings. However, that is not revival. Revival is when God comes on a community in all of His glory. Suddenly, the fear of God grips the entire community. That is what happened on the Isle of Lewis.

Before we begin our journey of revival on the Isle of Lewis, it is important to understand one thing. And we need to hear it from Duncan Campbell, himself, "I did not bring revival to Lewis. It grieves me to read or hear people talk about the man who brought revival to Lewis. I thank God I had the privilege of being there, and, in some small measure leading the movement for about three years, but God moved in the parish of Barvas before I ever set foot on the island." [5] Duncan Campbell once saw himself billed as "The Man Who Brought Revival to the Hebrides." He was extremely upset, and said that revival was a sovereign act of God, and that revival had come to the Hebrides before he ever arrived.

God had given Peggy Smith, the old blind lady, a vision. In prayer, she saw the church of her father crowded to capacity, packed with young people. She told her minister, Rev. James Murray Mackay, of her vision, and encouraged him to gather the elders and deacons of the church to pray. While seven men prayed in the north end of the parish in a tiny barn, Peggy and her sister, Christine, prayed in their humble little cottage in the south end of the parish. For three months they prayed, waiting on God. THEN, the fire fell that night about 2:00 in the morning in the barn among those seven men.

The Barvas church minister, Rev. James Murray Mackay, thought it would be a good idea for the church to hold a ten-day mission (a special series of meetings). But, who would he call to preach at these special services? Rev. Mackay went to a convention in Edinburgh. He met Dr. Tom Fitch. This was the same man who preached the night Duncan Campbell was so distraught about his spiritual life. Dr. Fitch told Rev. Mackay that Duncan Campbell was available to preach in the Highlands and the Western Islands.

When Rev. Mackay returned home, he went to see Peggy and Christine Smith. Peggy told her minister that God had given her another vision. God had revealed to Peggy Smith, not only that revival was coming, but the identity of the human instrument He would use in this revival. God even told Peggy the name of the man, Duncan Campbell. Peggy Smith told her minister that God had told her Duncan Campbell would be at the Barvas Church in a fortnight (two weeks).

Rev. Mackay found out that Duncan Campbell was preaching on the Isle of Skye. He sent word, asking him to come and preach a ten-day mission at the church in Barvas. Duncan Campbell sent back word that it was impossible for him to come. Campbell was making plans for a holiday convention to be held on the Isle of Skye. He sent back word to Rev. Mackay that he could not come, but he would try to come the following year.

Rev. Mackay told Peggy Smith the bad news, Duncan Campbell could not come. Peggy Smith replied, "That's what man says. God has said otherwise! Write again! He will be here in a fortnight."

In a matter of a few days, the Tourist Board announced that it had secured all of the accommodations for a week of festival celebration during the same period Duncan Campbell was preparing the holiday convention. Campbell felt it was necessary that he cancel the plans for the convention. Within a fortnight, Campbell was on board a ferry crossing the Minch, heading for the town of Stornoway on the Isle of Lewis.

When Duncan Campbell stepped off the ferry at Stornoway, he was met by the minister, Rev. Mackay and one of the elders of the church at Barvas. When Campbell stepped up to the minister and elder, they noticed he was wearing a heavy pair of black boots and a coat several sizes too large for him. The elder asked Duncan Campbell, "Mr. Campbell, might I ask you a question? Are you walking with God?"

Campbell replied, "Well, I can say this, at any rate, I fear God." Rev. Mackay told Campbell he was to address a meeting at the church at 9:00 that night. The minister said it would be a very short meeting, just an occasion to introduce Campbell to the congregation. There had been nothing in the newspapers, no handbills, no publicity of any kind about this special series of meetings. But, God had something in mind!

The meeting began at 9:00 that night. They sang some Psalms, had prayer, Campbell spoke for a bit. Campbell pronounced the benediction and the people filed out of the church and stood in the front yard. They stood there in a tense silence, waiting. Campbell was walking up the aisle toward the front door of the church. Rev. Mackay was beside him. Kenneth Macdonald, the deacon, who had prayed that night in the barn, "O God, are my hands clean? Is my heart pure?", came up to Campbell and said, "Mr. Campbell, God is hovering over us, and He is going to break through in a mighty move." Kenneth Macdonald was walking down the aisle with Duncan Campbell when he suddenly fell to his knees in the aisle, and began to pray. Campbell said he heard Macdonald pray, "God, you can't say that! God, you can't say that!" Again, Kenneth Macdonald fell into a trance. At that moment, the church door came open. The session-clerk came rushing in, and said, "Come to the church door and see what is happening." Campbell said he went to the front door and saw a crowd of at least 600 people. There had been less than 300 in the church service. Where had all these people come from? Some had come from a dance, as they had fallen under conviction. Others had streamed out of their homes across the village, drawn by the captivating power of Jesus Christ. Campbell suggested they sing a Psalm. It was announced they would sing Psalm 126.

When Zion's bondage God
    turned back,

As men that dreamed were we.
Then filled with laughter was our mouth,
    Our tongue with melody:
They among the heathen said, The Lord
    Great things for them hath wrought.
The Lord hath done great things for us,
    Whence joy to us is brought.
As streams of water in the south,
    Our bondage, Lord, recall,
Who sow in tears, a reaping time
    Of joy enjoy they shall.
That man who, bearing precious seed,
    In going forth doth mourn,
He doubtless, bringing back his sheaves,
    rejoicing shall return.

The crowd began to come back into the church. The building could not accommodate them. About one-half the crowd had to remain outside for lack of space inside the building. Inside the church, the place is packed. People were sitting in the aisles, in the window sills, on the pulpit steps. Campbell tried to make his way to the pulpit, but could not reach it for all the people. There was a young lady lying on the floor near the pulpit, a school teacher who had been at the dance when God swept in. Campbell heard her crying out, "O God, is there mercy for a sinner like me?" That school teacher found mercy, and went on to serve as a missionary in Nigeria. [7]

Campbell tried to preach, but, finally, saw it was a futile effort. People were praying, crying out to God for mercy, so Campbell just stepped aside and watched God work in the lives of the people.

About 3:00 in the morning, Campbell decided to go home. He was staying at the home of the minister of the church. The minister, James Murray Mackay, went home with Campbell. Duncan Campbell said, "We just left the church filled with people, crying out to God. We left them for God to deal with. God is the supreme counselor. They might not find God that night, nor the next, nor next week, nor next month, but, if they are seeking God with all their hearts, they will find Him. We gave no invitation. We did not say, 'Come to Jesus and be happy.' A person under deep conviction of sin is not happy." [8]

On the way to the minister's house, Campbell met a young man, not a Christian. He told Campbell that all the people who could not get inside the church had gathered at the police station. The young man wanted Campbell to go to the police station because there were so many in deep distress, and, the young man said, "And, I am in distress myself." Campbell started walking toward the police station. It was an extremely dark night. He heard someone praying beside the road, crying out to God for mercy. Campbell left this person beside the road, to find his way to God. He did, too. A few years later this young man beside the road became a minister.

When Campbell arrived at the police station, he found over 300 people standing, kneeling, crying out to God for mercy. Campbell spoke to them for a bit, then went home.

Now, why the police station?. Why did all these people choose that place to gather? The reason: next door to the police station lived the two elderly Smith sisters, Peggy and Christine. The people had gathered at the seat of divine power. THE GLORY OF GOD HAD COME TO THE ISLE OF LEWIS!!

This first meeting at the Barvas Church lasted from 9:00 P.M. until 4:00 A.M. God just seemed to move in. It might be well to mention that, during the Lewis Revival, no appeal was ever given, no invitation was extended. On the Isle of Lewis you could not mention an appeal. The church people of Lewis were Calvinists in their theology. If anyone made an appeal, or gave an invitation, the people would immediately say that this was man's work, not God's. However, the people of Lewis found out that when God moves in great revival, every corner becomes an inquiry room, every action becomes an invitation from the Living God.

From this first meeting at the Barvas Church, it just seemed a power was let loose that spread across the Island of Lewis. The following headline appeared in the newspaper, "The Spirit of the Lord was resting wonderfully and graciously on the different townships the following morning. You could feel His presence in the homes of the people, on meadows and moorland, and even in walking the public roads. God appears to be everywhere."

Why here? Why did God visit, in this most dramatic way, the

Isle of Lewis? Of course, there was the absolute sovereignty of Almighty God. However, there were human factors that we could consider. The people of Lewis had not lost their belief in the authority and inspiration of the Holy Word of God. They still believed that the words of the Bible were true, and, that those Words were divinely inspired by God Himself.

Another factor was the knowledge of the Bible that the people of Lewis possessed. The Bible was taught in the schools. Family worship was a tradition followed in almost every home, whether the people in that home were saved or not. Almost every home had family worship, morning and night. The children and young people in those homes had such respect for their parents, that they would join in the time of family worship. Duncan Campbell said, "Families learned the Word of God, and when the fire falls, the Word in the mind becomes the incarnate Word in the heart. God becomes real." [9] Children and young people were required, in the home, to learn the Shorter Catechism. The Shorter Catechism is made up of 107 questions concerning the teachings of the Bible. The answer to each question is recorded, along with scripture verses that pertain to the question and answer. Every child, in every home was required to memorize the Shorter Catechism. So, the people of Lewis were well-grounded in the teachings of the Bible.

Another factor was the familiarity that the people of Lewis had with revival. Revival had visited this island for the past two hundred years, about every 30 to 40 years. There were many people on the Isle of Lewis who recognized revival when it came, and they pursued it with all their hearts.

The next night there were fourteen buses at the Barvas Church. Word had spread across the Island of Lewis that revival had come. One of the buses came over sixty miles from the village of Leverburgh on the south end of the island. The majority of the people in the buses were lost people , and God swept into the buses.

A few years after the revival broke out in the church at Barvas, a young lady was standing to give her testimony in St. George's Cross Tabernacle in Glasgow, Scotland. She was going out as a missionary to Sudan, in northern Africa. In her testimony, she said, "I have very little to offer my Loving Redeemer, but, what there is, He has it all." 10

This young lady was saved during the Lewis Revival at the Barvas Church. Her testimony is quite remarkable. She was a student in school in the town of Stornoway. There were five girls in the school who were close friends. Four of the girls decided to ride a bus to Barvas, and attend the church services. The four young ladies tried to get the fifth girl to go with them, but she wanted nothing to do with it. She was dating a young boy, and was going to a dance with him.

The four young ladies boarded the bus. There was not one saved person on the bus, as it made its way to the church services at Barvas. Between Stornoway and Barvas, the bus driver suddenly pulled to the side of the road, stopped, and said, "I can't take you farther." he slumped over the steering wheel, gripped by God, and began crying out to God for mercy. God filled the bus, and everyone on the bus began to pray and ask God for His mercy. The bus stayed on the side of the road for three hours. They finally reached the Barvas Church at 1:00 in the morning. Services were still going on. Everyone on the bus was saved that night.

When the four girls arrived back in Stornoway, they went to the fifth girl's room, woke her up at 3:00 in the morning. She was quite unhappy to be awakened at that hour. But, as she listened to the four girls, and looked into their eyes, she said she saw something that could not be explained on the basis of the human. She gave herself to the search for what they had, and, the following night, she was saved at the Barvas Church. This young lady married the boy she was dating. He became a medical doctor, and the two of them spent their lives as missionaries in Thailand.

One evening, four young men climbed on a bus. All four of them were drunk. The young lady driving the bus was a friend of theirs. For some time she had been running around with the four young men, but the young lady bus driver had been saved at the Barvas Church. When they climbed on her bus, drunk, she said to them, "I am so sorry to see you in this condition." One young man said it was the look in her eyes that gripped his heart. He turned to the other three and said they would not go to the bar, but they would go to church. They were all four saved by 2:00 that night. Three of the four became ministers.

While the revival continued at Barvas, it leaped to the parish of Ness, on the north end of the Island of Lewis. One night, word came to Duncan Campbell that the church at Ness was crowded at 1:00 in the morning. Campbell was requested to come and speak. He, and some other ministers arrived at Ness to find the Holy Spirit moving among the people. The church was packed, people standing outside. When the church service was over, those who were interested in being saved were invited to a home for further instruction. In the Lewis Revival, these home meetings after the church services were called, "kitchen meetings." Usually Duncan Campbell would speak from John 10:27- 28 at these kitchen meetings, "My sheep hear My voice; I know them, and they follow me. I give to them eternal life, and they shall never perish."

The kitchen meeting at Ness dismissed at 3:00 in the morning. Someone told Campbell of a crowd of people who were out in a field, singing Psalms and praying. They had been unable to get inside the church. Campbell went out to the field and found a crowd of about 300 people. He spoke to this crowd of people. About 4:00 in the morning, a cottage door opened. The elderly lady who lived there came out. She said, "I wish you people would go home and allow people to sleep." An elder she had addressed told her, "Woman, get away home. You've been asleep long enough." [11]

While walking home from Ness, Campbell saw something that deeply impressed him. A man was lying on the ground. Three girls, about 16 years of age, were kneeling by him. One of the girls said to the man, "The Jesus who saved us last night can save you now." The girls saw that man saved as he lay there on the ground. [12]

It was in the parish of Ness that a most unusual thing happened one night. Duncan Campbell was asked to come to a farmhouse to preach. He walked seven miles to this house, arriving between 1:00 and 2:00 in the morning. The house was filled with people. Campbell began to preach to them. Suddenly, the back kitchen door opened and several men came in. It was evident they were not there to worship God. Campbell said their faces expressed demon possession. The moment these men walked in, Campbell found himself completely fettered and bound, unable to continue preaching.

Standing near Duncan Campbell was Kenneth Macdonald, the

man who had prayed that marvelous prayer in the small barn the night the fire of God fell. Campbell looked at Kenneth Macdonald, and said, "The devil is in this meeting. Satanic power has been let loose. You deal with it. You pray." Kenneth Macdonald began to pray, and prayed for twenty or thirty minutes. He stopped praying, looked toward heaven, and said, "God, will you excuse me for a minute. I want to address the devil? Devil, you are in this meeting, and you are here to frustrate the purposes of God. I now take upon myself, on the basis of the atoning sacrifice of Jesus, to order you out of this meeting. Devil, I put the blood of Jesus between you and this meeting. Be gone, devil." At that moment, the power of God fell on that farmhouse meeting, and men were gloriously saved, including all the wicked men in the kitchen. 13

As if turning lights on in a darkened room, the Isle of Lewis suddenly was thrust into the light by the coming of revival. The roads would be black with people, walking to church, walking to prayer meetings. Hearts were set aflame. Songs of praise filled the lips of people all over the island. The glory of God filled the Isle of Lewis.

So many wonderful stories have come out of the Lewis Revival. Stories of individuals whose lives were changed by the Master.

One of those stories has to do with a young lady, Faye, and her close friend, Christiann. Faye was excited about a school concert that was coming up in a few days. Then, news came to Faye that her friend, Christiann, had been converted at the meeting the night before. Faye was thunderstruck. She had no understanding what had happened to her friend. Faye went to see Christiann. She took one look at Christiann. Her face was shining. She seemed to be utterly transformed. Faye said, "You've got it!"

Christiann replied, "Faye, dear, you are so blind. It's not it at all. It's Him! The Lord Jesus Christ!" Faye began to cry.

The next day Faye went to Barvas, to her friend's house. This family wrapped their arms about Faye, and with hugs and tears streaming down their faces, they said, "Faye, have you come for the Lord to have mercy on you?" They began a prayer meeting, and prayed for Faye. Faye said, "They sent for John Murdo Smith, who lived next door. John Murdo began to sing and pray. They just laid everything aside and spent the whole afternoon. I started thinking of my emptiness and desolation, when they were all so full." 14

That evening, time came for the church services. They all went
to church. The church was packed, and the people began singing, "Set
ye open unto me, ye gates of righteousness." It seemed that every
word sung was pointed straight at Faye. She began to sob. Duncan
Campbell preached from the Song of Solomon. He preached about
the walls and hindrances that separate us from God. Faye knew those
walls were in her life. She didn't know what all the walls were, but
she knew they were there.

Duncan Campbell said, "You are sitting here right now,
thinking, "But, I do pray." That is what Faye was thinking of that
moment, that she did pray. Campbell asked, "But, what do you pray
for?" Faye thought to herself, "Well, I pray for God to make me
good." Campbell said, "You are asking God to make you good. If God
could make you good, why did the Lord Jesus Christ have to come
into the world? What a prayer you are praying! God cannot answer
it." Faye sat there thinking. The only prayer she had and the preacher
said it was a blasphemy. At that moment, Faye believed she was
totally without hope.

Duncan Campbell then said that Jesus came to place a bridge
over this terrible gulf, to demolish this terrible darkness, and bring us
back to God. He said that the Lord Jesus came to set us free. Faye
then wondered why she had not understood all of this, when she knew
it all so well. At that moment, Faye was set free from her sins.

During the course of the revival, without warning, darkness fell
across Duncan Campbell. For three months, he got little sleep. He
spent much of his time pacing the floor, weeping and praying. The
only time he had any relief during this period was when he was
preaching. The power of God would come over him, and he would
feel the presence of the Lord. However, as soon as he would return to
his room, the darkness would shroud his life again. After three
months, one night Campbell was praying, when a voice came to him
and said, "I can trust you now." Peace came to Campbell's heart, and
the darkness was gone.

No one but God knows of the impact that the two, old Smith
sisters had on the Lewis Revival. One day, Peggy, the 84 year-old,
blind sister, called for Duncan Campbell to come to her cottage. She

told Campbell that God had revealed to her that he should go to a certain village and preach. This particular village had stood in opposition to the revival. The people of this village had stated they did not want to get involved.

Duncan Campbell told Peggy Smith that he had felt no leading to go to that village. She replied, "If you were living as near to God as you ought to be, He would reveal His secrets to you also." Duncan Campbell took this as a Word from the Lord.

He asked Peggy if they could spend a little time in prayer together. As they prayed, Peggy Smith prayed, 'Lord, you remember when you told me this morning that in this village you are going to save seven men and they will become pillars in the church. Lord, I have given your message to Mr. Campbell, and it seems he is not prepared to receive it. Lord, give him wisdom, because he badly needs it."

After an hour or two in prayer, Duncan Campbell told Peggy Smith that he would go to this village. Peggy said, "You had better."

Duncan Campbell went to the village and found a crowd of 400 people waiting. The people were not sure why they had come to this place. They couldn't explain it. They were all standing in front of a house. The house was crowded to capacity, and others were standing in the yard, and in the road.

Campbell announced his text, "The times of this ignorance God winked at, but now commands men everywhere to repent, because He has appointed a day in which he will judge the world in righteousness by the Man he has ordained." (Acts 17:30) Campbell had only preached a few minutes when a man came out of the house and said to Campbell, "Mr. Campbell, come to the end of the house, there is a remarkable scene there. The most notorious characters in the community are on their faces, crying out to God for mercy. Campbell went into the house, found seven men in a back room, crying out to God. He spoke to them on his favorite text, "My sheep hear my voice, I know them, and they follow me. I give to them eternal life, and they shall never perish." (John 10:27-28) These seven men became elders in the church in that village. [15]

I find it totally impossible to describe real revival on a sheet of paper. The atmosphere seems to glitter with divine life. Everything seems to cry out that God is present. No wonder, on a day when the Pharisees asked Jesus to rebuke his followers for praising Him, Jesus said, "I tell you that, if these should hold their peace, the rocks would immediately cry out." (Luke 19:40)

When great spiritual awakening comes, the rocks, the grass in the fields, the clouds, all cry out, "God is present." In the Lewis Revival, a hardened sinner was sitting at a table, and began watching a fly buzzing around a lamp. He watched this lowly insect for a time, then muttered under his breath, "If you go any closer, you'll get burned." These thoughts flashed across his soul, he saw the danger facing his own soul, and began to seek the Lord.

During the height of the Lewis Revival, a ship was sailing close to the shore of the Isle of Lewis. The captain of the ship was lying in his bunk reading a dirty book. As the ship sailed closer to shore, suddenly, the captain was gripped by the power of God, fell from his bunk to his knees, and cried out to God to have mercy on him. This captain became a Brethern minister. [16]

God has such a wonderful way of getting people together to accomplish His will. He speaks to one person here, another person there, and then, the glory of God is revealed.

Early one morning, Duncan Campbell was traveling down the road on his motor bike, on the east side of the Isle of Lewis. It was 5:00 in the morning. He was on his way to visit a minister whom he had known in college in Edinburgh. This man was minister in a parish where revival had not yet come.

On the way to this minister's home, Duncan Campbell saw a young woman kneeling beside the road, weeping. He could tell she was in deep distress. He went by her about one hundred yards, stopped, turned his bike around, and went back to her. Campbell asked the young lady if he could help her. The young lady replied, "No man can help me."

Although it was a common sight, in those days of revival, to see someone kneeling and praying beside public roads, Campbell saw an urgent need in this young lady. He knew it was not exactly the proper thing for him to be alone, talking to a lady beside the road, but, Campbell felt God would have him talk to her.

Campbell took out his New Testament and began talking to her about Jesus Christ. She looked at Campbell and said, "You mentioned Jesus. He is dearer to me than the sons of men. As the apple tree among the trees of the forest, so is my Beloved." Campbell immediately recognized that she was speaking from the Song of Solomon, and felt he was in the presence of a young lady who knew God.

Campbell revealed to the young lady who he was, a minister who had been preaching in the revival at Barvas. The lady said, "O, I knew God would not fail us." Then she told Campbell her story.

Two young girls from this parish, both age 15, had gone to the revival services at Barvas, and had been saved. When they came home, they had come to this young woman who was kneeling beside the road because they knew her to be a converted lady. The three ladies decided to begin a prayer meeting. They covenanted together to pray two nights a week, Tuesdays and Fridays, in a little barn. So, these three young women, one, twenty-five years of age, and two girls, fifteen years of age, began to pray.

They had been praying for several months for revival to come to their parish. On the night Duncan Campbell found this young lady beside the road at 5:00 in the morning, God had given them the assurance that revival was coming.

Duncan Campbell suggested that the two of them pray beside the road. The two of them prayed for three hours, kneeling on this country road.

After three hours of prayer, Duncan Campbell traveled on to the house of the minister he wanted to visit. When he arrived at the house, the minister was completely astounded at what was happening in his parish. That morning, as Duncan Campbell and the young lady had been kneeling in prayer beside the road, a group of fourteen young men had gathered in front of the parish hall to discuss the amount of whiskey they should bring to a concert and dance on Friday night. As they discussed this, one of the young men said, "Boys, I think we should increase the amount of whiskey, because I have a strange feeling that this is the last time whiskey is going to come to this parish."

Another of the young men said, "Angus, surely you are not suggesting that revival is coming, that we are going to see what they are seeing on the other side of the island?"

Angus replied, "I don't know what is happening, but something is happening in my heart right now." He fell to his knees in front of the parish hall and began to cry for mercy from God. Within one hour, all fourteen of the young men had been saved.

Duncan Campbell remained in this parish for six weeks, preaching the gospel. He said it was like being in the midst of glory.

Duncan Campbell returned to this parish fourteen years later. On Saturday evening, the minister of the church called Campbell and asked if he would preach the next morning. When Campbell arrived at church on Sunday morning, he found the church crowded, not because he was preaching, for no one knew he was coming.

When church services were over, the minister asked Duncan Campbell to come to the vestibule of the church to meet the elders of the congregation. There were eleven elders, and ten of them were those young men who were saved in front of the parish hall as they discussed the amount of whiskey to bring to a dance. [17]

Duncan Campbell received a call to come to a parish on the Isle of Lewis where revival had not yet come. He knew the young minister and his wife quite well. The young minister asked if Campbell could come and preach in Communion Services in his church. When Duncan Campbell recalled past attitudes in this parish to revival, he could not resist accepting this invitation.

The former minister of this church had been bitterly opposed to the revival on Lewis. In fact, he had announced from the pulpit that if Duncan Campbell came to his parish, he would sic the dogs on to him. God removed this man from the pulpit, and now this young minister is leading the parish.

One night this young minister and his wife were getting ready to go to bed. He asked his wife, "Do you think we are ready to begin this ministry? I don't know how you feel, but my conviction is that we are not ready. Surely God can do more for me, more in me. I wonder if, together, we are walking with God?" That night they knelt beside the bed, and, at 2:00 in the morning, God did something to both of them that let God loose in the parish.

Duncan Campbell came to preach at the Communion Services in this parish church. Now, Communion in the Hebrides Islands is vastly different from what we are accustomed to in America. Communion begins on a Wednesday and, usually concludes on Sunday. There are services each day and each evening. When it is Communion season, work stops, schools close, shops shut their doors. Everyone concentrates on God.

Wednesday is the Pre-Communion Prayer Service. Thursday is fast day. People give themselves to waiting upon God. Friday is the men's meeting. The men are asked to give their testimonies. On Saturday, the people appear before the ministers and, they must give a testimony of having been saved by sovereign grace and must live accordingly. Those who pass this examination are given a token to sit at the Lord's Table. Then comes Sunday! There are usually five sermons on Sunday; the Action Sermon, the Sensing of the Table, making it clear who ought to be at the table, and who ought not to be at the table, a sermon before the sacraments are administered, a sermon following the sacraments, and, last, a sermon of guidance, comfort and strength to God's people.

At this parish church where Duncan Campbell had been invited, suddenly, during the Action Sermon, the fire of God fell. It became impossible to administer the Lord's Supper because of the distress of the people. Finally, they finished with the Communion, and the benediction was pronounced, and the people filed out of the church.

In a little bit, the people began to file back into the church. Duncan Campbell stood, and announced a text, "Who is this that cometh from Edom, with dyed garments from Bozrah? This that is glorious in his apparel, traveling in the greatness of his strength? I shall speak in righteousness, mighty to save." (Isaiah 63:1) However, preaching was impossible. The power of God just swept over the whole congregation.

The young minister and Duncan Campbell stood in the pulpit, just staring out at what God was doing. The young minister turned to Campbell and said, "O, bless God! This is Barvas all over again."

They were in the church for four hours. No one moved. Most of the time there was just a tense silence, occasionally there would be a cry of distress. Campbell heard one man cry out, "O, hell is too good for me!"

The people finally went out to eat the evening meal, then back into the church they came. Campbell preached, and announced the benediction. No one moved to leave. The young minister finally went to the back door of the church, indicating that the service was over. No one moved! He came back to the pulpit and asked Duncan Campbell, "What are we going to do?" Campbell told the young minister, "Do you remember the night you were converted? You remember that we were in the church for five hours and people were unwilling to leave. I got up and told the people they had been there for five hours. There were farmers there who had been away from home all day, and their cows needed milking. I told them, 'Perhaps you would like to go out for a breath of air, then, if you so desire, come back into the church." Campbell reminded the young minister that the people did go out, but came back into the church in a few minutes, and at 5:00 in the morning this young minister was saved.

Campbell encouraged the young minister to tell his people to go out for some air, but, if they desired, to come back into the church. In ten minutes the church is crowded again.

That meeting continued until 5:00 in the morning. Campbell said he could not say how many were saved during that night. He just felt that was a record that was kept in heaven. Word came the next morning that the fire of God had spread to an adjoining parish.

That is revival! That is true spiritual awakening! When God really moves among people you don't have to wonder about it. You don't need to advertize it! God takes care of His own publicity.

One of the most awesome stories of revival, and one of the most familiar stories to come out of the revival on the Isle of Lewis, happened at the small village of Arnol. Arnol is three miles south of the village of Barvas. The revival had its beginning in Barvas, had spread north to the village of Ness. All this time there had been severe opposition to the revival in Arnol. It seemed no one wanted to have anything to do with the revival. The main reason for their opposition had to do with doctrine. They felt that Duncan Campbell's talking about the baptism of the Holy Ghost was not according to the confession of faith of their church. Duncan Campbell proclaiming that there was an experience that could bring you into a large place with God. Ministers came from all over the island to the village of

Arnol to hold a position meeting. It was in the month of May, 1950, the crowds were going to these meetings, very few were coming to hear Duncan Campbell preach.

An elder came to Duncan Campbell and said there was only one thing to do, give themselves to prayer. This elder found a little meeting house, and about thirty gathered to pray. The prayer meeting was very difficult. Quite a number of the men prayed, but the prayers were stiff and formal. There was no vision, no fire in the prayers.

Between midnight and 1:00 in the morning, Duncan Campbell asked John Smith to pray. John Smith was the blacksmith from Barvas who had spent three months in the little barn in Barvas with six other men to pray. John Smith was there the night the fire of God fell in that little barn.

At this little meeting house in Arnol, John Smith started praying. He prayed for about thirty minutes, then stopped. He raised both hands toward heaven, and prayed, "God, do you know that Your honor is at stake? You promised to pour water on those who are thirsty, and floods on the dry ground. God, I don't know where Duncan Campbell stands with you. And, God, I don't know where these other men stand with you, but, if I know my own heart, God, I am thirsty and you promised that you would pour water on the thirsty and floods on the dry ground. O, God, if you don't do it, how can I believe you again? O   God, on the basis of Christ's atonement, I challenge you to fulfill your covenant engagement and do it now. God, Your honor is at stake."

At that moment, the meeting house where they were began to shake. Some of the men who were there thought it was an earthquake, but, it was the fire of God falling on that village.

Immediately, Duncan Campbell pronounced the benediction. Campbell put it this way, "I knew that God had taken the field." All the men walked outside. It was now past 2:00 in the morning. As they walked out, they saw the whole community coming alive. Lights began to shine in houses. Men came toward the meeting house. Women came, carrying stools and chairs, asking if there was room for them in the meeting. The Arnol Revival broke out, and what a visitation of God it was. The drinking house of that village closed that night, and never reopened. That night, Duncan Campbell was tired and thirsty. He went into a near-by house to get a drink of milk. He found nine women on their knees in the kitchen, all of them crying out to God. One of those women who was saved that night composed some of the most beautiful Gaelic hymns that they are still singing today. The following Sunday, Duncan Campbell looked out the window of the house where he was staying, and the road was black with people, walking to church. [18]

In the Arnol Revival, there was a sixteen-year old boy saved. His name was Donald Macphail. I will tell the story of Donald Macphail at a later time, but I want the readers to remember this name. Duncan Campbell said he never met anyone closer to God than little Donald Macphail.

So, God visited Arnol, a little village on the west side of the Isle of Lewis. The whole village was changed. Today, there are more people attending prayer meetings in Arnol than attended Sunday morning services before the revival came. What an experience, when God comes down!

Duncan Campbell received an invitation to preach the closing sermon at a convention in Bangor, Ireland in 1951. This was the second year of the Lewis Revival.

Campbell was sitting on the stage the night before he was to preach the closing sermon. Suddenly, he felt a deep impression from the Holy Spirit. He heard the voice of God, inside, saying, "Go to Bernara, and go immediately."

At the southwest corner of the Isle of Lewis is the small island of Great Bernara. It only had a population of about 500 people. Duncan Campbell had never been to Great Bernara. He did not know anyone on the Isle of Great Bernara, but God told him to go to this island.

Campbell went to the chairman of the convention and told him he must leave. The chairman asked, "When?" Campbell replied, "Right now. The Holy Spirit has told me to go." The chairman reminded Campbell that he was to preach the following night, but Campbell told him he had no choice but to obey God.

The next morning Duncan Campbell flew to Glasgow, then caught another plane to Stornoway, had someone drive him to the southwest corner of Lewis, where he boarded a little boat to take him to the Isle of Great Bernara.

When Duncan Campbell stepped onto the dock on the small island, there was a small boy about eight or nine years old standing there. He asked the boy to go to their minister and tell him that Duncan Campbell was on the island. The boy replied, "We don't have a minister. We have two churches, but neither one has a minister at this time. Elder Hector Mackennon is in charge of the church, and he lives in that house there on the hill."

Campbell told the boy to go tell Elder Mackennon that Duncan Campbell is here, and if he asks what Duncan Campbell, tell him the Duncan Campbell of the Lewis Revival. The little boy ran off, up the hill, came back in a while, and said, "Elder Mackennon said to tell you he was expecting you. You are to stay with his brother, and Elder Mackennon has already called a meeting at the church at 9:00 tonight, and you are preaching."

Later, Duncan Campbell found out, from Elder Mackennon's wife, the full story. The previous day, while Duncan Campbell was in Bangor, Ireland, Elder Mackennon, the island postman, had spent the day in prayer in his barn. Three times, during that day, his wife went to the barn door and heard her husband praying, "God, I don't know where he is, but You know. God, send him to us." At 10:00 at night, Elder Mackennon felt a peace settle over him, a peace that God had heard his prayer. That was the same time Duncan Campbell had heard the voice of God, telling him to go to Bernara.

Duncan Campbell made his way to the little church that night. The church was located just outside the village, up a hill. They had a very ordinary service. They sang some Psalms, had some prayers, and Duncan Campbell preached. Nothing unusual happened.

Duncan Campbell pronounced the benediction. The people were walking down the little hill toward the village. Campbell and Elder Mackennon were standing on the front porch of the church, watching the people. Elder Mackennon suddenly took his hat off, stood at attention, and said, "Mr. Campbell, stand! God has come!" Duncan Campbell looked down the hill and saw the people falling to their knees by the roadside, into the heather, crying out to God for mercy.

As the people were able, they got up and made their way back to the church. This service lasted until 5:00 in the morning. Duncan Campbell could only be on this tiny island for five days because of a previous preaching engagement, but he said it was five days of glorious revival. In fact, Campbell said there was not a home on the island where someone was not saved.

An island gripped by God! In following years, Duncan Campbell thought about a great fact we all need to consider. He was thankful that he was near enough to God to hear Him in Bangor, Ireland. What if Campbell had not been walking with God? What if Campbell had been out of touch with God, and had not heard His voice, telling him to go to Bernera.

Ah, but, that elder, Hector Mackennon. THE POSTMAN OF BERNERA! It was this man's habit to go daily to a certain place to pray. Every day he would go to the seashore, behind a big rock, and meet with God. This was one man who fulfilled the conditions of II Chronicles 7:14, "If my people, who are called by my name, shall humble themselves, and pray, and seek my face, and turn from their wicked ways; then will I hear from heaven, and will forgive their sin, and heal their land." [19]

The preceding event happened on the Isle of Great Bernera, which is on the southwest coast of the Isle of Lewis. South of the Island of Lewis and Harris is the island of Berneray.. One of the most unusual happenings of all of Duncan Campbell's ministry happened on the island of Berneray.

The year was 1951. It was the second year of revival in the Hebrides Islands. Duncan Campbell was invited to preach Communion Services on the Isle of Berneray. He found preaching so difficult, so hard. There was no revival on this island at all.

Campbell called a weaver in Barvas, a man who knew God, a man who knew how to pray. Campbell asked this weaver if he could get some of the praying men of Barvas and come to Berneray to pray. Campbell told the weaver, "If you can, bring little Donald Macphail with you." Donald Macphail was a sixteen-year old boy who had been saved in the revival at Arnol. He was a praying young man in whom Duncan Campbell had much confidence.

The praying men of Barvas came to Berneray and brought little Donald Macphail with them. The service began that night. Campbell felt fettered and bound in his preaching. He looked down to the front row of pews and saw Donald Macphail sitting there, weeping, the floor in front of him wet with tears. Duncan Campbell said he knew Donald Macphail was nearer to God than he was. Campbell stopped preaching, and said, "Donald, I believe you are nearer to God than I am. I want you to pray."

Little Donald Macphail began to pray. He prayed for twenty to thirty minutes, when, all of a sudden, he stopped praying, lifted his hands toward heaven, and said, "God, I seem to be gazing in through an open door." That morning their devotional had been from the Book of Revelation, when the Apostle John was gazing into heaven as if through an open door. Donald Macphail continued to pray, "I seem to be gazing in through an open door. I see the Lamb in the midst of the throne with the keys of death and hell." At this point Donald Macphail is sobbing his heart out. He lifted his hands back to heaven, and said, "My God, I see power there, let it loose!" He said it a second time, "My God, I see power there, let it loose!"

When Donald Macphail prayed this the second time, THE FIRE FELL! Duncan Campbell said he could never explain the physical manifestations that occurred. Campbell said what happened next was the only time in his ministry he ever saw this. All the people on Campbell's right threw their two hands into the air, toward heaven, fell back in their pews, and remained that way for two hours. All the people on the Campbell's left just slumped into each other, and into the pews and stayed that way for two hours.

God swept in! In a small village five miles away, at the same time, God swept through this little village. There was not a house in this village, five miles away, where someone was not saved while Donald Macphail was praying.

At the same time, in a ship, sailing down the minch, a sailor was in his bunk. He was arrested by God, was saved, and became a minister in the Brethren Assembly in England. A husband and wife were saved that night. On the same night, their daughter, who worked in a hospital in London, was on her way home, and was suddenly gripped by God and was saved.

Four miles north of the village of Barvas is the village of Borve. During the Lewis Revival, a family by the name of Macarthur lived in Borve. Mr. Macarthur was the local schoolmaster. Mr. And Mrs. Macarthur had six children. Two of the sons were named Allan Ian and Jack. Into the life of this family, God came. None of the family knew God, but God used different people and unusual circumstances to turn this family to Himself.

Th revival was burning bright in Barvas. There was a concert and dance scheduled on a Friday night at a meeting hall in the town of Carloway, about fifteen miles south of Barvas. One of the Macarthur sons, Allan Ian, was to serve as the Emcee for that dance.

That night, the bus loaded up with young people, going to the dance in Carloway. As the bus passed the Barvas Church, it was full of light, and full of people. Allan Ian Macarthur played his accordion loudly as they passed the church, thinking, perhaps, it might drown out everything that was going on in church. He was one of the young people who didn't want this going on in their community. Many people were afraid of revival, afraid it would be an end to some of their entertainment, afraid it would mean an end to their way of life. Allan Ian Macarthur was one of those who was afraid.

While the bus was traveling to Carloway to the dance, the two young men who were to play their bagpipes at the dance, were in Barvas. One of the pipers, William Smith, had finally given in to the pleadings of his mother to go to the church meeting. But, he was determined to go to the dance. But, that night, William Smith heard the voice of the Lord. He didn't want to follow the Lord. He wanted to go to the dance, but happily, he found the Lord that night in a little house just west of the church. It was in the kitchen meeting, after church services were over. William Smith and the other piper went to the kitchen meeting, and were saved.

At the kitchen meeting that night were Rev. Murdo Maclennon and his wife. Rev. Maclennon was minister of the church in Carloway. When he saw that the two pipers, who were to have played at the dance in Carloway that night, were saved, Rev. Maclennon turned to his wife and said, "Look, there are the two pipers who were to play at the dance in Carloway tonight. There they are crying for mercy. Let's go to the dance and tell them what has happened."

The first half of the concert/dance was a series of skits, songs and accordion playing. They had just finished this first half, and were clearing the floor to begin the dance, when the back door of the meeting hall opened, and in walked Rev. Murdo Maclennon and his wife. Allan Ian Macarthur, the emcee of the dance, became very angry. He had been drinking. He walked up to Rev. Maclennon and asked, "Have you paid to get in? Do you have a ticket?" Rev. Maclennon replied, "I have a ticket that will take me anywhere." Allan Ian Macarthur said to him, "Well, it won't take you in here until you pay for it. And, besides, you had no right to sneak in the back door."

Allan Ian started for the minister, but one of his friends held him back. Allan Ian thought, "Well, we will just let him have his say, and that will be the end of it."

Rev. Maclennon said to the crowd, "When I was walking up to the building, there was a young lady singing. She had such a beautiful voice. I would like for her to come forward and sing two verses of a Psalm with me. The girl didn't want to do it, but Allan Ian Macarthur's mother, Annie, was present. She encouraged the young lady to sing with the minister. When they began singing, most of the crowd joined in. They were singing Psalm 139 in the Gaelic language:

> From thy Spirit whither shall I go?
>   Or from thy presence fly?
> Ascend I heaven, lo, thou art there;
>   There, if in hell I lie.
> Take I the morning wings, and dwell
>   In utmost parts of sea;
> Even there, Lord, shall thy hand me
>   lead,
>   Thy right hand hold shall me.
>
> If I do say that darkness shall
>   Me cover from thy sight,
> Then surely shall the very night
>   About me be as light.
> Yea, darkness hideth not from thee,
>   but night doth shine as day;
> To thee the darkness and the light
>   Are both alike alway.

While the song was being sung, Allan Ian Macarthur felt something was happening to him. He didn't know what it was. Rev. Maclennon began to pray. God swept into the meeting hall. Allan Ian went to the minister and apologized for the things he had said, then left the hall. He went out to the bus, sat down, and began to weep and weep. His mother came out to the bus and tried to get him to come back inside. He told her he couldn't, that God was dealing with him.

When God swept into the meeting hall, the dance was over. The hall emptied. The young people got on the bus and started for home. Mrs. Macarthur told the young people, "When we were coming to the dance, there was a lot of carrying on. Remember, some of you are not going home the same as you came to the dance. We need to be quiet, going home." On the ride home, there was stillness and quietness on the bus.

The next morning, Saturday, there was a quietness and stillness in the Macarthur home. Jack Macauthur, the eleven-year-old brother thought someone must be ill or someone had died. Jack's sister told him, "I think Allan Ian was converted last night." Jack had no idea what she was talking about. Jack said, "As the day went on, I became aware that something very significant had happened. There was something very strange in the atmosphere."

That Saturday morning, Mrs. Macarthur went into Allan Ian's bedroom to see how he was doing. He told his mother that God had been dealing with him and something had happened to him.

That Saturday evening, all the family was in the sitting room. Jack Macarthur remembers his father and mother looking at each other. His father asked, "Where's the Bible?" Mrs. Macarthur went to a cupboard, got the Bible out of its case, the first time it had ever been removed from the case. Mr. Macarthur read a passage from the Bible, then said the Lord's Prayer. That was the first time that had ever happened in this home.

At this time, Jack Macarthur was eleven years of age. He could never remember being inside a church. Shortly after this experience in the Macarthur home, church-going became a part of that family's life. Jack Macarthur said, "This totally transformed my childhood. It wasn't long after that that Duncan Campbell was staying with us, having a mission based in our own home. He came to preach next door. He lived with us for several weeks. This was in the pre-electricity days. I would go every day, three-quarters of a mile down the road, with two gallon tins to get paraffin, so there would be light for the lamps for the meeting that night. I went to the meeting every night. I can't remember much of what he said, but there was an awareness on an 11-year-old night after night of God searching me. I was afraid of what would happen each night. I just continued to struggle with God. At that stage, people were being converted each night, and in the house meetings afterwards. I did manage, for several weeks, to just push it away from me. But, a deep, lasting impression was made on my own soul. My conscience became very tender. While I was not converted until the following year, I thank God for those nights." [20]

It was not long until Mr. Macarthur was really praying. Jack Macarthur remembers, "A new dimension had come into our home. It didn't matter where people were; in New Zealand, in Argentina, at sea, every night they were remembered with a consciousness. Without a telephone, communication was being made with someone who loved them. Our home had changed. Someone new had taken charge. Father was totally transformed." [21]

Allan Ian Macarthur and Jack Macarthur later became ministers. They served their lives as pastors, one on the Isle of Lewis, the other in Glasgow.

I traveled to the Isle of Lewis in October, 2001. Never have I had a more thrilling experience, than to walk the land where revival occurred. I found myself, at times, floating on air, and, the next moment, my knees would crumble under me.

To have the privilege of interviewing several elderly people who were saved in the great Lewis Revival was beyond belief. To talk to people like Donald John Smith, Donald Macleod, and Mary Murray was the privilege of a lifetime. I will have more to say about these dear people in a later chapter.

On the Isle of Lewis I got to see where many of these events took place. Donald John Smith, a resident of Shader, showed me all of the places of interest. Donald John Smith is 79 years old. He was saved in the Lewis Revival. To drive around with this dear man and look upon those places; the barn where the seven men prayed and the fire fell, the Barvas Church , where God came in power when Duncan Campbell preached, the police station where hundreds of people gathered, crying out to God for mercy, the location of the little cottage of Peggy and Christine Smith, the elderly sisters who waited on God until He came in power.

While I was on the Isle of Lewis, my wife and I drove from Stornoway, where we were staying, to Barvas, to attend church. On the Hebrides Islands, churches have their mid-week prayer meeting on Thursday evening. We arrived at the church at 6:40 P.M. We entered the church, sat on the back row, and waited for the beginning of service, which was 7:00 P.M. At five minutes until seven, an elder came down the aisle, leaned over to me, and asked, "Are you a minister?" I replied that I was. He said, "We don't have a minister tonight. Will you preach?" I thought I might faint. To think, that a farm boy from western Oklahoma would have the privilege and honor of preaching in the Barvas Church, where God showed His hand so mightily. It was an evening I will cherish forever.

CHAPTER EIGHT

Soldiers in a Common Cause

Soldiers fight! They fight because there is a great need, because they have been commanded to fight. As I write these words, the military men of the United States are fighting a war against terrorism in the nation of Afghanistan. This war is a result of the horrible tragedy of September 11, 2001 when the World Trade Towers in New York City and the Pentagon in Washington, D.C. were destroyed.

God's soldiers are also commanded to fight, but the rules of engagement are totally different from that of the world. The Apostle Paul wrote, "Fight the good fight of faith, lay hold on eternal life, whereunto you are also called, and have professed a good profession before many witnesses" (I Timothy 6:12). Also, when Paul was speaking concerning a soldier in God's army, he said, "You therefore, endure hardness, as a good soldier of Jesus Christ" (II Timothy 2:3).

There were many good soldiers for Jesus Christ during the revival on the Isle of Lewis during the years 1949-53. They fought the good fight because there was a tremendous need. They fought because they had been commanded to do so by their commander, Jesus Christ. They also fought because they had a glimpse of what victory was like.

To single out some of these "soldiers in a common cause" is quite difficult. I am fearful that I will exclude some. No one can adequately write of all those soldiers, for they are too numerous to mention. However, I want to call your attention to some who had an uncommon call to do battle in the work of the Lord.

DUNCAN CAMPBELL

When you think of the Lewis Revival, your mind is immediately drawn to this Highland, Scottish preacher, Duncan Campbell. He was the son of a Highland crofter and stone mason, grew up on a farm in the Black Crofts area of Scotland, converted to Jesus Christ at the age of fifteen, served his country during World War I, then came home to spend a life in service to the living God.

It is quite natural to mention the name of Duncan Campbell first, however, Campbell, himself, abhorred the fact that many credited the Lewis Revival to him. He always played down his part in the revival. He gave credit for the revival to two things; to those who preached the Word of God across the years, before he arrived on the island, and those who gave the time to wait on God in prayer. Christians seem to always be discussing the possibility of revival. When does revival come? How does it come? Duncan Campbell placed great importance on prayer in revival. During his stay on the Isle of Lewis, when Duncan Campbell would encounter opposition, he would always call together a group of men who knew how to pray. Campbell said, "More was wrought through the prayers of these men than all the ministers put together, including myself." [1]

The revival on Lewis did not begin when Duncan Campbell arrived on the island. There was already a mighty moving of God in a small barn, and in a tiny cottage in the village of Barvas.

Campbell attributed his part in the Lewis Revival to one thing; a baptism from God. He had a spiritual hunger for something more from God, and the Holy Spirit filled his life that night in the upstairs study in the manse at Falkirk.

To be sure, Duncan Campbell had an important part in the Lewis Revival. He came to the island filled with the Spirit of God, ready to be used. Some, on the island, were impressed with the attitude of Duncan Campbell when he came. The forms of worship on the Isle of Lewis were different than on the mainland of Scotland. Churches had their particular way of doing things. There was no instrumental music, no hymns. They sang only the Psalms. When Duncan Campbell came to the island, he did not try to change things. He became one of the people of Lewis. He adapted to their forms and styles of worship. He totally identified himself with the spirituality of those who had already known revival.

There was great opposition to the revival in parts of Lewis. The opposition had to do with theology. Many were opposed to Campbell's insistence on the baptism of the Holy Spirit as a definite experience after conversion. More opposition came because of the continuing war between the doctrines of Calvinism and Arminianism. Most church people in Scotland were strict Calvinists. Calvinism taught the doctrines of sovereign grace, election, and predestination. Arminianism taught the doctrine of free choice, that man could choose to be a follower of Jesus Christ. Duncan Campbell was accused of being an Arminian. One minister on the Isle of Lewis wrote, concerning the Lewis Revival, "The teachings given were thoroughly Arminian and the methods followed those of the typical Arminian revivalist, with great insistence upon immediate and unqualified profession of conversion." [3]

Jack Macarthur, who was saved during the Lewis Revival, and served his life as a minister of the Church of Scotland, said, "Duncan Campbell was accused of being Arminian. He was the least Arminian preacher I have ever heard." [4]

What kind of man was Duncan Campbell? He was a man easy to know, delightful to be around. Rev. John Murdo Smith said, "Duncan Campbell impressed me as a man who, like Enoch, walked with God, and was a man who walked in the will of God, and it was so easy for God to use him." [2]

Duncan Campbell was a tall man, good-looking. He was an extremely forceful preacher. In fact, one night, Campbell struck the pulpit so hard that he broke a bone in his hand. He was fervent in preaching the gospel of Jesus Christ.

One thing I have found quite unique in the preaching of Duncan Campbell. Of all the sermons I have gathered of Duncan Campbell over the years, the vast majority of his sermons are based on Old Testament texts. I do not mean to say that he never preached from the New Testament, but most of his preaching came from the Book of Psalms and Isaiah. There was a triune theme in the Lewis Revival. Most of the preaching in the church services had to do with sin, judgment, and hell. But, when it came time for the "kitchen meetings", those meetings held in homes after the church services were over, Campbell would almost always turn to his favorite Scripture in dealing with people who were under conviction, "My sheep hear My voice. I know them, and they follow me. I give to them eternal life, and they shall never perish, neither shall any man pluck them out of My Father's hand" (John 10:27-28). Out of this text, Duncan Campbell, the man who had just preached with such power and thunder on sin, judgment, and hell, would approach those who were under conviction, and share with them a loving Shepherd, who was speaking to them, wooing them, calling them to Himself. Often the fire of God would fall when Campbell taught seeking sinners about this Savior who loved them deeply.

PEGGY AND CHRISTINE SMITH

These were two, elderly sisters who lived next door to the police station in Barvas. Their home was a tiny, quaint cottage, but no home has ever been more filled with the power of God than this home. Peggy was eighty-four years of age, and blind. Christine was eighty-two years of age, and bent over with arthritis.

In my study of the Lewis Revival, I feel these two women had more to do with the coming of revival to this island than any other persons. I realize there were many involved, many praying, many seeking after God. But, Peggy and Christine Smith were the ones who urged prayer upon others, who pled with others to wait on God.

When the minister of the Barvas Church came to the Smith home to read the declaration of the Presbytery, it was Peggy Smith who urged the minister, Rev. James Murray Mackay, to gather the elders of the church together to pray. It was Peggy and Christine Smith who devoted two nights a week, from 10:00 to 3 or 4 o'clock in the morning to pray for revival.

It was to Peggy Smith that God revealed Himself on several occasions. God gave her a vision that revival was coming, that the church of her father's would be crowded with young people. It was to Peggy Smith that God gave a message for Duncan Campbell to go preach in a village where there was great opposition to revival.

Only eternity will reveal what these two, simple, wonderful sisters meant to the Kingdom of God as they entered into a ministry of prayer on the Isle of Lewis.

DONALD MACPHAIL

As we look at the "soldiers in a common cause", we move from two elderly sisters who were in their eighties, to a young, teen-age boy, who was used in a mighty, awesome way during the Lewis Revival.

Donald Macphail was fifteen years old when he was converted to Christ during the Lewis Revival. Duncan Campbell went to the village of Arnol to preach. Arnol had stood in great opposition to the revival at Barvas because of Campbell teaching on the baptism of the Holy Spirit. God broke through in Arnol at a prayer meeting one night in a little meeting house. John Smith prayed a unique prayer, and the small meeting house literally shook.

The night after this prayer meeting, Donald Macphail was saved. He had heard at school about the revival in Barvas. The young people at school referred to the revival as "the plague." The night after the meeting house shook, Donald Macphail went to the services more from curiosity than anything. That night, he heard God's voice, went outside, and began crying, "I want Christ. I need to get right with God." The night after he was saved, Donald Macphail brought his mother to the services. He walked his mother to a certain spot, and said, "Mother, this is where Jesus saved me yesterday, and he can save you now." 5 His mother was saved that night. The next night he led his father to salvation in Christ.

Two weeks after Donald Macphail was saved, he was out in the field among the heather and the cattle. He began to pray out in the field. After some time, he was baptized with the Holy Spirit. It came time for the evening meal at the home. Donald's parents became worried about him. Some people went out to search for young, Donald Macphail. They found him face-down, among the heather, praising God in Gaelic.

Duncan Campbell heard about this experience that Donald Macphail had. He went to the Macphail home to talk to Donald. His mother said he was out in the barn, in his usual place, praying. When Duncan Campbell opened the barn door, he saw Donald Macphail on his knees in prayer. Donald looked up, saw Duncan Campbell, and said, "Mr. Campbell, would you excuse me for a bit? I'm having an audience with the King." 6

During the revival on the Isle of Lewis, Duncan Campbell was invited to go to the small island of Bernera to preach communion services. Berneray is south of the island of Lewis. At this time, revival had not come to Berneray. In fact, Duncan Campbell said that, on the island of Berneray, the stream of vital Christianity was running low. Campbell began the communion season. He found preaching almost impossible. The services were cold, dead and wooden. Campbell got in touch with the praying men of Barvas, and asked them to come to Berneray and pray. Campbell said, "If possible, bring little Donald Macphail with you." 7

A small group of men from Barvas arrived on the island, along with Donald Macphail. On Friday night, Duncan Campbell stepped into the pulpit to preach. He found preaching so difficult that he stopped. He looked down on the front row, and saw little Donald Macphail, sitting there with tears streaming down his face. Campbell said the floor was wet with his tears. Campbell said, "Immediately, I knew that boy was nearer to God than I was." [8]

Duncan Campbell told the congregation that he was finding it extremely difficult to preach. He looked at Donald Macphail and asked him to pray. Donald Macphail prayed for about twenty minutes, and then stopped......" Then, Donald Macphail said, "Lord, I seem to be gazing in through the open door." That morning, at family worship time, they had been reading the biblical account from the Book of Revelation when John saw the vision of the open door. Now, Donald Macphail is praying, "Lord, I seem to be gazing in through the open door. I see the land with the keys of death and of hell." Macphail stopped praying and began to cry. When he was able to control himself, he suddenly lifted his right hand to heaven and cried out, "My God, I see power there, let it loose! My God, I see power there, let it loose!" When Donald Macphail said these words the second time, the fire of God fell into that church.

Duncan Campbell never tried to explain what happened next. He said it was the only time he ever saw this in his entire ministry. The only explanation Duncan Campbell would give, was to say that God was in it.

When little Donald Macphail prayed, "My God, I see power there, let it loose!", every person on Duncan Campbell's right lifted their two hands toward heaven and fell back in a trance. Their hands were up in the air for two hours. On the left side of Duncan Campbell, every person just slumped into each other, fell over in their pew. They stayed that way for two hours.

And, what a transformation! There was not one single person who was in the church that night who was not saved within one week.

But, the remarkable thing that happened on the Isle of Berneray was not what happened in the church that night, but what happened outside the church. Five miles away from the church was a little village. Not one person from this village was in the church service that night, but when this remarkable manifestation took place in the church, the fire of God fell on that village five miles away. There was no preacher, no church service, no organization, nothing but God. In that village, five miles away, there was not a single house where there was not someone saved, that night.

During the Lewis Revival, Duncan Campbell received a letter from a communist who lived on the Isle of Lewis. He was an avowed atheist. He invited Duncan Campbell to come to his home. When Campbell arrived, the atheist asked him, "Can you prove to me, logically, that there is a God?"

Campbell replied, "I wouldn't attempt to do it, because you do not discover God by logic. The Bible says, 'The world by wisdom knew not God.' If you wish to meet the God I believe in, and the God who is real to me, spend one-half day in the village of Arnol."

Later, the atheist told Duncan Campbell, "Did you say half-a-day? Half-an-hour did it! I met little Donald Macphail yesterday." In meeting Donald Macphail, this communist/atheist had met God, and was saved.

When this teen-age prayer warrior, Donald Macphail, grew up, he became a missionary. He spent his life telling the good news of Jesus Christ in the nation of Yemen. Today, in retirement, Donald Macphail is back at home, living in the village of Arnol on the Isle of Lewis.

JOHN SMITH

Of all the men on the Isle of Lewis, John Smith is one of the most unique, exciting men about whom I have read. He was a blacksmith who lived north of the Barvas Church, in the little village of Shader.

It was John Smith who prayed that powerful, challenging prayer that night in Arnol. In that little meeting house, around 1:00 in the morning, Duncan Campbell asked John Smith to pray. He stood to his feet, holding his cap in his hand, and prayed, "God, did you know that Your honor is at stake? God, you promised to pour water on him who is thirsty, and floods upon the dry ground. And, God, You're not doing it! God, I don't know how Mr. Campbell stands before you, and I don't know how these other ministers stand before you, but, God, I'm thirsty! God, if you don't pour water on us, how can I ever trust you again?' THEN, the fire fell! That little meeting house literally shook. Revival came to the village of Arnol.

It was this unknown blacksmith who prayed that prayer. But, he was no stranger to prayer. John Smith was one of the seven men who had gathered in the little barn in Barvas to first pray for revival. He was there that night when Kenneth Macdonald prayed and the fire of God fell in that barn. Prayer had become a way of life for him.

When I was visiting in Barvas, I had the opportunity to visit, at length, with Donald John Smith, a retired shop-keeper from Shader. He told me he was in a prayer meeting one night at the home of John Smith, the blacksmith, when, in the middle of the prayer meeting, a dove flew in and lit on the shoulder of John Smith.

Did that happen? Is it possible that is real? Well, God is real! Prayer is real! And the same Holy Spirit that descended like a dove on Jesus, at His baptism, is the same Holy Spirit who visited the Isle of Lewis in a most remarkable way.

When I think of John Smith, the Shader blacksmith, I immediately think of what Paul wrote, "Because the foolishness of God is wiser than men; and the weakness of God is stronger than men. For you see your calling, brothers, how that not many wise men after the flesh, not many mighty, not many noble, are called; But God has chosen the foolish things of the world to confound the wise; and God has chosen the weak things of the world to confound the things which are mighty; And base things of the world, and things which are despised, has God chosen, yea, and things which are not, to bring to nought things that are; That no flesh should glory in his presence." (I Corinthians 1:25-29)

To think, that Almighty God would reach down to an obscure blacksmith, who lived in one of the most remote places on the face of the earth, and that Almighty God would visit with power, love and majesty. What a man was this Shader blacksmith!

OTHERS

How can I tell of all the others, unnamed people who lent their lives to the Lord during this time of great revival? The men and women, the young people who prayed and sang, who went to barns, and behind rocks at seashores to wait upon God for mighty revival.

No one today can tell the name of the butcher who would pray and pray until his body shook with the very power of God. Nor do we know the name of the crofter who would go to God in prayer, clenching his fists as if he were a boxer, and would command the devil to leave a church service. Nor will we know, until heaven, the name of the tweed-merchant who would use his old, grey truck to carry people from one meeting to another, all over the island.

We would do well to remember the countless housewives who would open their homes, night after night, for kitchen meetings that would last all night long. They never complained about damage to their home.

My own heart becomes cheerful when I read of young boys and girls who would march along the seashore at 4:00 and 5:00 in the morning, singing hymns to Jesus Christ, that they had written themselves.

All of these were soldiers in a common battle. There were so many who fought a good fight, who kept the faith, who finished the course.

CHAPTER NINE

The Characteristics of the
Lewis Revival

Every revival throughout church history has had certain characteristics which identify it. The Moravian Revival of 1727, the revival under John Wesley and George Whitefield, the Welsh Revival of 1904, all had certain characteristics which rose to the surface.

The Lewis Revival was no different. It, too, had characteristics which made the Lewis Revival what it was. It is interesting that God uses different things with different people. God speaks in unusual ways to make sure His message is heard. "The wind blows where it will. You hear the sound of it, but cannot tell where it comes from, nor where it goes, so is everyone who is born of the Spirit." (John 3:8). Let's take a look at the outstanding characteristics of the Lewis Revival.

SPIRITUAL ATMOSPHERE

The predominant characteristic of the Lewis Revival was the overwhelming presence of God. He was everywhere! People could not get away from him. When the fire of God would fall in a parish, the community would just come alive with the presence of God. Everything seemed to speak the name of Almighty God. To the people of Lewis, God was present in the heather, the rocks, the clouds. The spiritual atmosphere was electric with the Lord. That presence of God fell upon people as the fear of the Lord. The fear of God would settle on a community as the dew of the morning. Without any warning, a whole community would suddenly be gripped by God.

If revival is anything, it should be this; a time when the presence of God is among us to convict, to guide, to stir, to renew. Henry Ward Beecher was once looking back on his past, and remembering God's mercy toward him. Beecher said, "I recall three or four instances in which it seemed to me that if certain occurrences had not taken place just as they did I should have been overthrown. If I had not been taken out of Boston at one time, as I was, I do not see what would have prevented me from going to destruction. I look back upon passionate moments, upon moments of wilfulness, which would have led me to worse disaster, had not events in the providence of God transpired to check me in my course and change my career." [1]

Spiritual atmosphere does that. It takes lives that are aimless, and gives them guidance day by day. On the Isle of Lewis, men would be bowed over their looms, weaving tweed; women in their homes, cooking meals; young people walking along the roadside, when they would be so overtaken by the presence of God, they would find themselves lying prostrate on the ground.

It was for this very reason Duncan Campbell was able to make his statement, "Seventy-five percent of those who came into saving relationship with the Lord Jesus Christ, came into that experience before listening to a sermon, or attending a place of worship." [2]

Perhaps the outstanding characteristic of the Lewis Revival was this: God was everywhere! There was spiritual atmosphere.

LIVELINESS

The people of Lewis are a reserved, dignified people. There sense of worship is quiet, reserved, without emotion. Before the fire of God fell on the Isle of Lewis, church services were dull, staid, and wooden. One of the converts of the Lewis Revival, a young lady named Mary Morrison said, "The spiritual temperature in the island before the revival was religious, but certainly not lively." [3]

But, when God came, the people came alive. Hearts were broken! Tears were shed! Crying out to God was heard! Singing was heard in churches, on roads, on buses. Everywhere people were singing praises to God, and talking about Him.

There is nothing wrong with healthy, God-directed liveliness. One time a group came from a church in Scotland to a meeting at which Dr. Govan was preaching. Dr. Govan was the founder of the Faith Mission. This group began shouting loudly, waving handkerchiefs. Finally, Dr. Govan found it impossible to preach. Later, Dr. Govan, Duncan Campbell, and Willie Lesley sat down to eat supper. Willie Lesley was an old man at this time. It was Willie Lesley who wrote some of our great hymns, hymns such as, "The Old, Old Story", "Life, Life Eternal', and "Lord, Send Us Revival." Dr. Govan asked Willie Lesley to lead in prayer before they ate. Willie Lesley prayed, "Lord, I would like to thank you for the young folks at the meeting. I would like to thank you for their enthusiasm, but, it must have grieved your heart to see so much of the steam that ought to have gone to the piston, blowing out through the whistle." [4]

When God came in power on the Isle of Lewis, there was enthusiasm, and emotion, and liveliness, but it was totally directed by the Holy Spirit.

SPIRITUAL SENSITIVITY

When real revival comes, souls become extremely sensitive to the Holy Spirit. People who are walking with God find their spiritual antennae reaching out to the gates of heaven for guidance, inspiration, and direction. Those near to God have intuitive feelings that can show them where to go, what to do, and to whom they should speak.

During the Lewis Revival, an unusual greeting was coined because of the spiritual sensitivity of the people. When people would meet each other, they would greet one another by asking, "Have you done business with God today?" People were irresistibly pulled to homes where prayer meetings were being conducted. Men, women and young people would find themselves drawn to a particular person, only to find that person earnestly seeking the Lord.

This spiritual sensitivity was expressed over and over again during the Lewis Revival. A weaver would be sitting at his loom, and become burdened for someone in the community. He would leave his loom, make his way to the neighbor, and find that neighbor in deep distress of soul. A bus driver, driving down the road, would suddenly become deeply burdened for his passengers. He would pull over and urge the passengers to come to Christ.

The characteristic of spiritual sensitivity was real and dominant in the lives of the believers on the Isle of Lewis. Because God was everywhere, His people were sensitive to Him.

Duncan Campbell was invited to go to Ireland to preach. During his sermon, he made this statement, "Calvary will not cover what you've got to uncover. He that hideth his sin shall not prosper." A man in the meeting got up and left when Campbell made that statement. The man did not return the next night, but, on the third night of the meeting, the man returned, and asked to speak to Duncan Campbell.

The man said, "I suppose you were surprised at me leaving the service in the middle of your address?"

Campbell replied, "Yes, I was a bit surprised."

The man then told this story, "I will tell you why I left. When you made that statement that Calvary will not cover what you've got to uncover, a little dog began to bark."

Campbell said, "I didn't hear a dog barking, and I don't think anyone else in the church heard a dog barking."

The man said, "When I was a little boy, I stole a puppy. I got five pounds for it, but no one in the community knew what had happened to this puppy, but I knew. I sold it to a farmer across the border. After several years, a preacher named Fletcher came to our community and I was led to profess faith in Jesus Christ. I had no thought of the puppy. Years went by and I became an elder in the Presbyterian Church. That was forty years ago. And I was never troubled until two nights ago when that puppy began to bark at the ear of my soul. I was so disturbed that I left the meeting, got in my car, and made for the farm where I stole the puppy. The farmer is dead, but his son was still living there. I told the son my story, then paid him for the puppy, with forty years of interest. I then went across the border. The farmer to whom I sold the puppy is dead, but I found his daughter, went to her and told her my story. I told her that, in heaven's sight, I was a thief." [5]

How wonderful it is when souls become sensitive to the leadership and convicting power of the Holy Spirit of God.. This spiritual sensitivity was like a cloud, overhanging the people of God throughout the Lewis Revival.

NO SENSE OF TIME

When revival came to Lewis, the sense of time, in the lives of people, vanished. There was no day, nor night. Weavers would spend twelve hours at their looms, from 8:00 in the morning, until 8:00 at night. Then, they would go to church services, later to a kitchen meeting, getting home at 4:00 or 5:00 in the morning. Farmers, housewives, students, shop-keepers would do the same.

One young lady from Barvas said, "Our house was open to meetings. We used to have meetings there all the time. My mother wasn't in the church service, but my father was. He was a church officer and an elder. I was in the church meeting, too. The minister said at the close of the service,'Now, we will have another meeting in about an hour in Mr. Macdougal's house just across the road. I rushed home and told my mother we had better get chairs and seats, for there was going to be a meeting in our house. That's the way it was. We had lots of meetings in houses, every night." 6

Margaret Macleod, a young person who was saved during the Lewis Revival, said, "We went to school every day. People worked in the fields every day, and then, every night we would go to church and stay until 3:00 or 4:00 in the morning. We never felt tired. The Holy Spirit not only took care of our spirits, but our bodies as well." 7

It was as if sleep were either impossible, or undesirable. Every night there would be groups who would gather on the public roads, or by the seashore singing praises to God, and telling each other what God had done for them.

I sometimes wonder if this is a sense of what eternity will be like. Those who know the living God, through our Lord, Jesus Christ, will one day live in a place where there is no night. Time will have vanished. Praise and fellowship will continue, forever and ever. That is a sense of what the people of Lewis felt.

THE GUIDANCE OF THE HOLY SPIRIT IN PREACHING

Duncan Campbell had always been diligent in preparation of his sermons. As a pastor, he spent hours studying, preparing what he would preach on Sunday. But, in the Lewis Revival he found his time so constricted, so full, that he had little, if any, time to prepare sermons. He would preach as high as seven times a day, never knowing, from day to day, where he would be preaching, nor to whom he would be preaching.

Many, many times as Duncan Campbell would stand to preach, he would announce a text that would speak directly to someone in the congregation. Many times Campbell had no way of knowing what was going on in the hearts of the people who were listening.

One night, a group of people made their way to a church meeting in a lorry (truck). Seven miles from the church, the lorry broke down. They found a boat, rowed across the loch, and got to the church with the service already in progress. Campbell stood and announced the text, "They also took shipping and came to Capernaum, seeking for Jesus." (John 6:24) This group of people who had rowed a boat to church, found Jesus Christ that night. 8

Another instance of the guidance of the Holy Spirit in the preaching of Duncan Campbell occurred in the life of a young lady, Mary Morrison. For some time, Mary had been under deep conviction. With some friends, she went to church services at Kenlochen one night. As they approached the church, Mary Morrison said, "Tonight Duncan Campbell will preach on the five foolish virgins." She felt like one of them. She had a lamp (Bible) in her hand, but was unprepared to meet God. As they entered the vestibule of the church, they heard Duncan Campbell say, "Turn in your Bibles to Matthew 25. Tonight we are going to meditate on the story of the foolish virgins."[9]

Duncan Campbell often preached the same sermon. One night he preached in one church, drove twenty miles to preach in another church. He saw an elder in the second service, who had also been at the first service. Campbell told the elder, "I am afraid you are going to have to listen to the same sermon again."

The elder replied, "Don't worry about that, Mr. Campbell. You just carry on. I'm an angler, and I would never dream of throwing away a fly the fish are taking."[10]

There is no doubt that the hand of God was on the preaching of Duncan Campbell. The Holy Spirit guided him to a portion of Scripture time and time again.

CONVICTION OF SIN

In any revival, conviction of sin will be one of its characteristics. The Lewis Revival was no different. There was a particular phrase used for this on the Isle of Lewis. When anyone on Lewis fell under deep conviction of sin, they were said to have "caught the curam."

Many times, Duncan Campbell would stop preaching because of the deep distress of the hearers. Campbell's voice would be drowned out with the sound of men, women and young people weeping. When this would happen, Campbell would usually step aside from the pulpit, and just stand and watch as the Lord did His work in the hearts of people.

One old man on the Isle of Lewis, who saw many under deep conviction, prayed, "Lord, now that You have us in the big pot, boil us well!" [11]

Sincere, God-sent conviction is a terrible thing to behold, and a horrible thing to go through. One feels at the end of mercy. Time after time, Duncan Campbell heard people, under deep conviction, praying, "God, hell is too good for me." There is a sense of hopelessness in conviction, an atmosphere of total lostness. This was one of the dominant characteristics of the Lewis Revival.

FEARLESS PREACHING

Duncan Campbell was an uncompromising preacher. There was nothing complex about his sermons. He preached on sin; what it does to a person, and where it will lead. He talked about living and dying without Jesus Christ.

As Duncan Campbell preached, he would stare at the congregation with a penetrating look. Sweat would pour from his body as he told the people about the way of life through Jesus Christ, and the way of death without Him. Campbell was no diplomat in the pulpit. He preached on sin, judgment, the wrath of God, and hell.

Campbell never thought, for one moment, of trying to be pleasing to people in his preaching. He preached a fervent gospel. It intrigues me that Duncan Campbell would preach sin, judgment, wrath, and hell in the church services; however, in the house meetings, afterward, when dealing with people who were seeking a Savior, Campbell would tenderly wrap them in the arms of the Good Shepherd, telling them of the love of God. Quite unique!

PHYSICAL MANIFESTATIONS

This is one characteristic of the Lewis Revival with which many people have a problem. People would fall to the floor (prostrations), go into trances, see visions, jerk their arms into the air and stay in that position for hours.

Duncan Campbell never tried to explain these physical manifestations. In fact, he never even tried to explain them, but, he did say that anyone who would try to associate these physical manifestations with satanic influence was coming very close to committing the unpardonable sin.

One time, during the ministry of George Whitefield, he began removing people from his meetings who would cry out, or fall down in the meetings. When he would have them removed, it seemed to put a damper on the meeting. Lady Huntington told Whitefield, "You are making a great mistake. Don't be wiser than God. Let them cry out; it will do a great deal more good than your preaching." [12]

One young lady on the Isle of Lewis repeatedly went into trances. In the trance, she would receive messages which she would pass on to Duncan Campbell. One night, in a trance, she saw a girl, twenty miles away, in great distress. She told Campbell. He immediately went to the home of the young girl, and found it just as he was told. During the revival, not one of the messages this young lady received in a trance proved false.

When I visited the Isle of Lewis, I spent several hours with an elderly man in the village of Shader. He showed me one house where the glory of God shone as a bright light one dark night over this house. He showed me another house where a dove appeared in the house during a prayer meeting.

Across the years, there have been many people who have given undue importance to these physical manifestations. It is important to remember that Jesus Christ was the central theme of the Lewis Revival, not the physical manifestations.

Concerning these manifestations, Jack Macarthur said, "We can't contain the presence of God. There were things that happened in physical manifestations among the most shy and the most quiet of people. There is a danger that these things are what catch people's attention. They can distract from that which happened; the revelation of Jesus Christ, alive, powerful and challenging. We look back and wonder why this came to an end. Why did the revival stop? It may be that the eye has gone to the gift rather than the Giver." [13]

Mary Morrison Peckham said, concerning these manifestations, "We saw physical phenomenon. They did happen, but they were not central. The awareness of the presence of God was central, the phenomenon was peripheral. The physical phenomenon was not distracting, because it was happening in an atmosphere of God." [14]

This last statement is a powerful one. Today, in our church services, some one can get up to leave the auditorium, and everyone looks at them. Just someone leaving is distracting. But, in the Lewis Revival people would fall to the floor, cry out in loud sobbing, lift their arms toward heaven for hours, but it was not distracting to the central thing that was going on, the revelation of Jesus Christ to the lost.

OPPOSITION

As far as I can tell, opposition is one of the chief characteristics of any revival. It was no different on the Isle of Lewis. Severe opposition rose in many parishes. The opposition came from ministers, elders, laymen and laywomen in the churches.

Duncan Campbell was attacked, often, for his teaching about the baptism of the Holy Spirit. Campbell lived his life in the overflow of the experience he had with God on the horse's back in France during World War I. He was firmly convinced that God had baptized him with the Holy Spirit. Since this was not according to the confession of faith of the Church of Scotland, Campbell aroused much opposition from those who did not accept this belief.

Opposition came from ministers and churches who accused Duncan Campbell of teaching and preaching Arminianism, that man had a choice to receive Christ as Savior. To a church society that had been stepped in Calvinism for so many years, the preaching of Campbell was difficult to take. However, listening to the sermons of Campbell, and reading his books, one would have a difficult time of accusing Campbell of being Arminian. One statement Campbell makes, over and over again, is this, "I believe in the sovereignty of God, but I do not believe in any sovereignty that nullifies the responsibility of man."

Campbell also had charges thrown at him concerning financial support during the Lewis Revival. During the revival one church donated an offering to the Faith Mission, of which Campbell was a part. Some made accusations that the Faith Mission was reaping benefits from the churches of Lewis. Duncan Campbell biographer, Andrew Woolsey, stated that he had, in his possession, a full list of contributions and expenses that Duncan Campbell kept during the Lewis Revival. At the end of each quarter, Campbell showed a deficit. [15]

Denominationalism was one source of opposition during the Lewis Revival. On the Isle of Lewis, at this time was the Church of Scotland and the Free Church of Scotland. One church accused Campbell of stealing members from one church to another. Some could not believe that revival had not come to their denomination. People became jealous of their own lives, and jealous of their own church. There were many who looked for revival, who longed for revival, but could not believe that when revival came, it did not come to their denomination.

To understand another aspect of the opposition, you need to understand the people of the Isle of Lewis, at that time. It was customary and expected for people to wear black clothing, black shoes, and somber looks to church. One event happened in this regard that made Duncan Campbell laugh and laugh, as he would tell this story, over and over again. One man who met Duncan Campbell said, "I was out for a walk yesterday and I met the plague. It isn't hard to see that there's no grace in him. You have only to look at his shoes, they were brown." [16]

When God comes in all of His power, opposition is to be expected. It is normal, else everyone would see revival. Some looked upon Duncan Campbell as a sheep-stealer, others looked upon him as the devil, himself. We must remember this! If there is no opposition, we should wonder if what we are seeing is really revival!

THE WORD OF GOD AS THE SWORD

Duncan Campbell always looked at the Bible as the very Word of God. One of the wonderful characteristics of the Lewis Revival was the work of the Word of God as a sharp Sword that cut through all the sin and rebellion, all the ignorance and preconceived ideas, and revealed the matchless love of Jesus Christ.

Campbell never underestimated the Word of God to do its wonderful work, but he avoided the danger of overestimating the work of Scripture. He felt that the Word of God could guide men to Jesus Christ, but it could never save. Only Jesus Christ could save a lost person.

Duncan Campbell had a motto concerning the Bible that he spoke, over and over again, "Preach the Word! Sing the Word! Live the Word! Anything outside of this has no sanction in heaven!" [17]

Duncan Campbell watched churches that had resorted to drama, dances, plays, movies, and other forms of entertainment. He abhorred all of this. One Christian leader asked Duncan Campbell what entertainment they had provided for the young people during the Lewis Revival. Campbell retorted, "Entertainment? They wanted no entertainment. Their desire was to hear the Word of God and attend the prayer-meeting." [18]

Duncan Campbell preached the Word of God. He did not believe the Christian life was a life of fun and games, but a serious battle, to be lived according to the Bible, and nothing else. He noted, as he preached, that people were crushed under the hammer of the Word of God, that hope began to shine forth through the Word of God, that life came through Jesus Christ, as He was revealed through the Word of God.

EXPECTANCY

As I have read through all the available material on the Lewis Revival, I have been constantly amazed at the atmosphere of expectancy that invaded the lives of those who walked with God. Through those years, 1949-53, those who waited on God in prayer, those who felt a cleanness in the air, those who lived near to the throne, lived on the edge of a clear confidence that something was going to happen. They came to the church services, expecting a visitation from God. They went to the kitchen meetings, expecting large blessings.

During that first service Duncan Campbell attended at the Barvas Church, he was keenly aware of the spirit of expectancy in the hearts of those who knew God was coming in great power; the crowded church, the Spirit-filled singing. Then, when the church service was over, all the people were reluctant to leave. They stood outside the church in a tense, still silence, waiting, waiting....sure that something was about to happen. Suddenly, Kenneth Macdonald gave out a shrill cry, and fell into the aisle of the church in a trance. The fire of God fell and the congregation flooded back into the building.

Oh, those people who expected this to happen; Rev. James Murray Mackay, Kenneth Macdonald, John Smith, Peggy Smith, Christine Smith, and the other four men who had met in a small barn for three months. They all expected God to come in power, and He did.

SINGING

I was pleasantly surprised to find that singing played a large part in the Lewis Revival. In fact, it was one of the chief characteristics of the awakening.

One needs to understand that church singing is different in the Hebrides Islands than we are accustomed to in American churches. Still today, there are no musical instruments, and no hymns are sung. They sing only the Scottish metrical versions of the Psalms.

One man from the Isle of Lewis said he had never heard, before or after, singing that he heard during the revival. He added, "I heard one Christian who has now gone to be with the Lord say that the Lord's presence was felt more deeply during the singing than at any other time during the revival. The singing during a service was an indication of the type of meeting we would have. I remember that in one or two services you felt you could continue singing throughout the whole service, and during the singing converts were born into the kingdom. Quite a number came through during the singing at the time of revival." [19]

During the time of revival, people were singing everywhere. They would be walking down the road, in groups, singing the praises of God. They would be singing on buses of public transportation. Praise to God filled the lips of the people of Lewis.

In every parish, singing was vastly important in the Lewis Revival. The first night, when the fire of God fell at Barvas, the people were gathered outside the church. They sang two Psalms as they stood in the churchyard in the presence of God.

I will not come within my house,
    Nor rest in bed at all;
Nor shall mine eyes take any sleep,
    Nor eyelids slumber shall;
Till for the Lord a place I find,
    Where he may make abode;
A place of habitation
    For Jacob's mighty God. (Psalms 132:3-5)

Singing moved from Barvas to Arnol. After John Smith prayed that night, the people all stood outside the little meeting house, singing praises to God:

When Zion's bondage God turned back,
    As men that dreamed were we,
Then filled with laughter was our mouth,
    Our tongue with melody. (Psalm 126:1-2)

I mentioned earlier concerning a group of people who were riding a lorry to go to a church meeting in the Parish of Lochs. The lorry broke down seven miles from the church. The people found an old row boat, rowed across the loch, arriving while church was in progress. All the people who rowed to church that night were saved. As they were getting back into the boat, to row back across the loch, the congregation gathered on the shore, and they all sang together:

When all Thy mercies, O my God!
    My rising soul surveys,
Transported with the view, I'm lost
    In wonder, love and praise.
O how shall words, with equal warmth,
    The gratitude declare
That glows within my ravished heart!
    But Thou canst read it there.
When nature fails, and day and night
    Divide Thy works no more,
My every-grateful heart, O Lord,
    Thy mercy shall adore.
Through all eternity to Thee
    A joyful song I'll raise,
For, oh! eternity's too short
    To utter all Thy praise.

Toward the end of the Lewis Revival of 1949-53, great revival broke out on the southern end of the island at Tarbert and Leverburgh. Perhaps more than any other place, singing played a great part in these two parishes. Wave after wave of deep conviction would sweep over the congregation, and men and women would bend before the Holy Spirit, crying out their prayers of repentance in the words of

Psalms 130:

> Lord, from the depths to Thee, I cried
>> My voice, Lord, do Thou hear;
> Unto my supplication's voice,
>> Give an attentive ear.
> Lord, who shall stand, if Thou, O Lord,
>> Should'st mark iniquity?
> But yet with Thee forgiveness is,
>> That feared Thou mayest be.

Along the southwest coast of the Isle of Lewis is the parish of Uig. This area is marked by beautiful cliffs and beaches. During the Lewis Revival, seven American ministers came to visit the parish of Uig. As they were walking through a valley, they heard singing. It seemed as if the singing was coming from every direction. They heard:

> His name forever shall endure;
>> Last like the sun it shall;
> Man shall be blessed in Him, and blessed
>> All nations shall Him call.
> And blessed be the Lord our God,
>> The God of Israel,
> For he alone doth wondrous works
>> In glory that excel.
> And blessed be His glorious name
>> to all eternity;
> The whole earth let His glory fill,
>> Amen, so let it be. (Psalms 72:17-19)

One of the ministers turned to the others and said, "This is heaven; heaven around us." That night revival reached its pinnacle in the Parish of Uig. [20]

Although only the Psalms were sung in church, the young people who were converted during the Lewis Revival wrote some of the most beautiful Gaelic hymns ever heard. Two of the young people who were saved during the Lewis Revival testified of the power of singing in their own experience.

Mary Morrison wrestled with God for months. But, on August 24, 1950, as she sat in the weekly prayer meeting, the truth of the gospel came into her heart, and she was converted. That night, at 2:00 in the morning, she and her friends walked along the seashore, singing:

> Now none but Christ can satisfy,
>> None other name for me!
> There's love, and life, and lasting joy,
>> Lord Jesus, found in Thee!

It was her final year in high school in Stornoway. The year was 1949. Faye was enjoying life, drinking in all the world had to offer, then the revival came. Many things happened that led Faye to a saving knowledge of Jesus Christ, but one of the most dramatic things happened during the singing of a hymn. The congregation was singing:

> Bearing shame and scoffing rude,
>> In my place condemned He stood:
> Sealed my pardon with His blood,
>> Hallelujah, what a Savior!

As they were singing that song, Faye suddenly focused on the words she was singing. Her voice stopped, tears came to her eyes. She realized she had been singing a lie. Jesus Christ was not her Savior.

Finally, one night in a service that Faye described as a time of singing of birds that it seemed like heaven upon earth, songs of deliverance as friends were saved, songs of praise for help in testings and trials, songs of penitence as one grieved the Holy Spirit through zeal without knowledge. Faye was gloriously saved, and has spent her life as the wife of a missionary doctor in the nation of Thailand.

But, Oh, heavenly singing! On the Isle of Lewis they heard it! Duncan Campbell said he only heard singing from heaven twice. One night, about midnight, he was walking down a country road with about twenty other people. Suddenly, heavenly music was heard by all of them. Some of the people on the road thought the end of the world was coming. Campbell said they were caught up in the Lord. Some had visions on the road that night. One young lad prayed, "O, Blessed Savior, my hand has touched your breast.' [21]

We should never underestimate the power of music in revival. It was one of the chief characteristics of the Lewis Revival, and it still speaks to our hearts today.

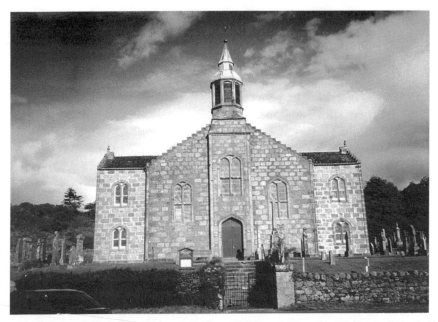

The Ardchattan Church on Achnacree Bay. Childhood Church of Duncan Campbell.

The childhood home of Duncan Campbell on Achnacree Bay in Blackcrofts Area. The Ardchattan Church is in the background.

The interior of the Ardchattan Church, childhood church of Duncan Campbell.

Interior of the Ardchattan Church. The segregated Lord's Table in the center.

Uniform of the Argyll and Sutherland Highlanders
World War I.
Duncan Campbell was a member of this unit.

The church at Ardvasar on the Isle of Skye. Duncan Campbell's first pastorate.

The Manse at Ardvasar. Duncan and Shona Campbell's first home.

Donald Angie Maclean and the author. Mclean was a missionary on the Isle of Skye for 33 years. A personal friend of Duncan Campbell.

The Manse at Falkirk. In the upstairs room on the right Duncan Campbell had his great experience of coming to a fulness of the Holy Spirit.

The church at Falkirk where Duncan Campbell was minister.

The interior of the church at Falkirk. The pulpit is the headboard of a bed.

Charles and Mary Ramsey in front of the Manse in Falkirk. Duncan Campbell married them here in 1941.

The author standing at the entrance to Barvas, Isle of Lewis. The Lewis Revival had its beginning here.

The landscape of the Isle of Lewis. The author's wife, Nancy.

Donald John Smith, the shop keeper of Shader who was converted during the Lewis Revival.

The Barvas Church, Isle of Lewis. The first church where great revival came.

The interior of the Barvas Church, Isle of Lewis.

The site of the small barn where seven men prayed for three months and the fire of God fell.

The Police Station in Barvas. The night the Revival came, hundreds of people gathered here. Peggy and Christine Smith's cottage was next door.

The home of John Smith, the Shader blacksmith who prayed one night in Arnol and the house shook.

The house in Barvas, where the two pipers were saved the night of the dance in Carloway.

The church at Shader, Isle of Lewis. Great Revival occurred here.

The home of Barbara MacDonald. During a prayer meeting, the Shekinah Glory of God shone on this house one dark night.

The home of the MacArthur family in Borve. This family was changed the night of the dance in Carloway.

The meeting hall in Carloway. Rev. Murdo Maclennon entered the dance and the Power of God fell.

The meeting house in Arnol. When John Smith, the blacksmith, prayed this house shook.

The Callanish Stones on the Isle of Lewis. Erected between 3,000-4,000 B.C. Thought to be either a prehistoric calendar or a pagan worship site.

Donald Macleod of the village of Arnol who was converted during the Lewis Revival.

Alex and Mary Murray of Stornoway. Mary was converted during the 1939 Lewis Revival.

Duncan Campbell, Christine Smith and Peggy Smith. Two elderly sisters who prayed until revival came. Christine was crippled and Peggy was blind.

The Gravestone of Rev. Duncan Campbell and his wife located behind the Ardchattan Church in the Black Crofts area of the Highlands of Scotland.

CHAPTER TEN

The Theology of the Lewis Revival

Every great revival throughout the history of the Christian church has been characterized by distinct doctrines of theology. It seems that each revival has had a particular doctrine, or doctrines that have risen to the surface. It could well be that God, in His infinite wisdom, has seen fit to emphasize a certain doctrine or doctrines for the good of the church in a particular time and location.

The Reformation of the early 1500's was borne and carried on the great doctrine, "the just shall live by faith." It was the theology of this verse of Scripture that moved Martin Luther toward the Lord, and, it was this doctrine that moved the church from the blackness of the Dark Ages to the light of the missionary movement of the church.

In the Moravian Revival of 1727, the awakening came on the wings of prayer. God came down on those blessed believers at Herrenhut after they had given themselves completely in a time of concentrated prayer.

During the revival in England under the preaching of George Whitefield, it seems God took this time to emphasize the doctrine of the new birth. It is said that George Whitefield preached on the subject, "Ye must be born again" over 500 times. Whitefield was once asked why he preached on this subject so much of the time. Whitefield replied, "Because, ye must be born again."

The revival in America under the preaching of Jonathan Edwards seemed to find its way on the preaching of the judgment and wrath of God. Who can ever forget reading the sermon of Edwards, "Sinners in the Hands of an Angry God." People in the pews would tremble and cry out as Edwards set forth judgment and the wrath of God on unbelievers.

When revival came to America in 1858, it was not in preaching, but in prayer that the revival came to fruition. Prayer meetings sprang up all over the nation, and people were drawn to Christ simply by prayer.

The Lewis Revival, in the Hebrides Islands, had its own emphases on different doctrines. The particular doctrines that rose to the top were not unusual, nor were they doctrines that had been lost through the years. It just seems as if they were doctrines that God chose to emphasize at this particular time.

As usual, the doctrines or theology of any movement finds its source in the preacher of the revival. The Lewis Revival was no different. Although the Church of Scotland held to many basic teachings concerning the Bible, Duncan Campbell came to the Isle of Lewis with his own particular brand of theology in some cases.

Duncan Campbell was not a trained theologian. Campbell looked on theology through a person's life. He wanted to know one thing, "Does it work?" Campbell knew, beyond a doubt, that God could save and change a life. Christ had worked in his life, and he had seen Him work in countless other lives. That was all Campbell needed. No matter how orthodox a person's theology was, if it did not mean a changed life, it was worth nothing to Duncan Campbell.

TOTAL DEPRAVITY

When Duncan Campbell came to the Isle of Lewis, he found a very religious people. They were well grounded in the Scriptures, most homes having family devotions twice every day. The Bible was taught in the schools, and the people were basically, very good people.

Campbell began preaching the total depravity of man. There was an effort on his part to get people to understand that being religious was not the answer.

As Campbell preached, he looked back over his own life, using that life as a measuring rod for his proclamation of the gospel of Christ. He remembered his distress of soul, his times of uncertainty, his wrestling within himself when he was a soldier in World War I. When Campbell was shot on the battlefields of France, he remembered lying there, the blood flowing freely, and he felt such a sense of unworthiness to go out and meet God. In his preaching, Campbell would mention, time after time, the inner depravity he felt in his soul, lying beside his dead horse on the battlefield.

It was to be expected that Duncan Campbell would preach on the depravity of the human heart, and, that the people of Lewis would be gripped by this doctrine, that normal man has come into the world with a propensity to sin. Man is depraved in his nature, and has to secure a new nature to be right with God.

THE LOSTNESS OF MAN

Duncan Campbell really believed that men, women, and young

people were lost without Christ. Wherever Campbell spoke, whether in church, in a home, on the street, he spoke plainly to remove false hope in religion. He would speak of the awful consequences of being lost without Jesus Christ.

Campbell was a plain-spoken man, in private and in preaching. On one occasion, he had preached on the lostness of man. After the service, a self-righteous women came to Campbell and said, "I don't need you to preach to me like that. I have been through the Bible myself." Campbell replied, "Perhaps so, madam, but have you allowed the Bible to go through you." [1]

Undoubtedly, the conviction Duncan Campbell had concerning the lostness of man without Christ, evolved from his dealings with the Lord in his upstairs study at the manse in Falkirk. That night God gave him a vision of thousands upon thousands of men and women lost without Christ. He never forgot that vision. In this vision he received from God that night when he came back to a fullness of the Holy Spirit, he saw multitudes of people marching into hell. This made such a penetrating impression on Campbell that he never forgot it, never wavered from preaching the lostness of men without Christ, and a hell for those who never came to the Blessed Savior.

THE SOVEREIGNTY OF GOD

When Duncan Campbell came ashore on the Isle of Lewis, he had come to a place where the sovereignty of God was taught, believed, and, in fact, was a way of life. The teaching of the Church of Scotland was that of Calvinism, total, complete, and without question.

The doctrine of the sovereignty of God became the doctrine of contention during the Lewis Revival. The opposition that arose, came because of this doctrine. Other ministers accused Duncan Campbell of being an Arminian, that he believed man had a free choice in accepting Christ as Savior.

Duncan Campbell was not an educated theologian. One could say that Campbell was a practical theologian. If your commitment to Christ worked, then it was right. He always looked at the practical aspect of your walk with Christ.

Campbell looked upon the school of thought that man can do

absolutely nothing, that everything is in the hands of the sovereignty of God, as impractical. Campbell believed in the sovereignty of God with all of his heart. But, when that view of the sovereignty of God becomes so strict that it eliminates man's responsibility, Campbell believed that bordered on heresy.

I have twenty-four audio tapes in my library of Duncan Campbell preaching. Time after time, on these tapes, Campbell makes this statement, "I believe in the sovereignty of God, but I don't believe in any type of sovereignty that nullifies man's responsibility." Although Campbell believed in the sovereignty of God, he believed whole-heartedly that God makes use of men.

In one of Campbell sermons, he is preaching on a passage of Scripture from Matthew 21. This was the occasion when Jesus told two of His disciples to go into a village, where they would find an ass, with a colt. He told the disciples to bring them both to Him. Then Jesus said, "And if any man say aught to you, you shall say, 'The Lord has need of them, and straightway he will send them." (Matthew 21:3)

Duncan Campbell was preaching on the need. He asked, "How was the need met?" Campbell said the need was met first, by the foreknowledge of God. Campbell said, "Oh, I believe in the sovereignty of God. I'm glad that my background is Calvinistic, but, He knew that there was an ass there to be used. He knew the day, He knew the place, and He knew the time." 2 Campbell believed that every man's life is a plan of God. He quoted a statement by a man named Boston, "Every born-again believer has God's work for him born with him." 3

Duncan Campbell seemed to follow the advice of A.W. Pink. In his book, The Sovereignty of God, Pink says that in a community where one aspect of the Divine sovereignty and human responsibility question has been particularly emphasized, it is necessary to place emphasis on the other side to secure a balanced approach.

In many places, Duncan Campbell would preach gladly and strongly on the sovereignty of God, but in the Highlands and the Hebrides Islands, which had been a stronghold of hyper- Calvinism for many, many years, Campbell preached on man's responsibility in his personal relationship to God.

Another aspect of the doctrine of the sovereignty of God in the Lewis Revival was the absence of any public appeal to come to Christ. In America, in certain churches, we are accustomed to a public invitation, to personal counseling. We train counselors to work with people who want to become Christians. This did not happen in the Lewis Revival. Campbell gave no public appeal, no invitations at the church services, nor would he counsel with a person under deep distress, for fear he would interfere with God bringing that person to Himself. It was not unusual for Duncan Campbell to leave a church service with the building fully packed , with people crying out to God under deep conviction of sin. Campbell felt quite comfortable with leaving people in the hands of God, whom he considered the Supreme Counselor. Campbell often said, "People under deep distress of soul may not find God tonight, or the next night, or next week, or next month, but he who searches for God will find Him, when he searches for Him with all his heart."

HOLINESS

The first church where the Lewis Revival broke out was the Barvas Church. The minister of that church was Rev. James Murray Mackay. He was later asked to address the General Assembly of the Presbyterian Church of Scotland in Edinburgh. In that address Rev. Mackay said this, "That night, when God swept into a prayer meeting and revival began, I made this profound discovery, that God- sent revival must ever be related to holiness and separation." [4]

When Duncan Campbell had the experience of a baptism of the Holy Spirit, while on a horses' back, during World War I, he said he felt as pure as an angel. Although Campbell was accused of believing in "sinless perfection", he never taught that doctrine, nor believed in it. He once heard a man say that he had not sinned in forty years. Campbell replied to the man, "Well, brother, you have just broken the record!" [5]

Campbell did not believe in a once-for-all cleansing, but believed we should walk in the light if we are to know continuous cleansing. Campbell preached that every Christian should walk in the Spirit, ever guarding against a choice of unclean things, always cultivating an attitude of total surrender to the known will of God.

In the Lewis Revival, holiness of life became the evidence that God had really done a work of grace in an individual's life. The Holy Spirit brought heart purity to the believer.

PRAYER

As important as preaching was to Duncan Campbell, prayer was equally important. He always attributed the Lewis Revival to the praying of seven men in a little barn in Barvas, and the praying of the two elderly Smith sisters in their humble little cottage.

Not only did Campbell believe in praying about the messages he preached, but he also felt that prayer was absolutely necessary to break down all opposition. To him, prayer brought victory.

Campbell spent hours in prayer. He had learned to pray as a teen-age boy at the Black Croft farm, in a little barn. Throughout his life, he found private prayer and family prayer essential.

For Duncan Campbell, the most important part of the day in prayer was early in the morning. Somewhere, Campbell had heard the advice Dr. Stuart Holden's mother had written in his Bible the day he was ordained. Campbell followed this advice, "Begin the day with God. See His face first, before you see the face of another." Over and over again Campbell would say in his sermons, "Give the best hours of the day to God."

On the fly-leaf of his own Bible, Duncan Campbell wrote the words of General Sir William Dobbie, "I have never found anything to compare with this morning-watch as a source of blessing, when one meets God before meeting the world. It is a good thing to speak to Him before we speak to other people, to listen to His word before we listen to the voices of our fellow-men." 6

The Lewis Revival was conceived in prayer, the prayers of seven men and two old ladies. And, the Lewis Revival continued in prayer. Men praying during the church services, at the weaving looms, working on the crofts; women praying in their homes, young people praying together and separately in schools and by the sea shore. Prayer became a way of life for the people of Lewis.

One minister said when he was inducted into a church on Lewis in July, 1951, Duncan Campbell came to be with his church in December. The first few nights were very hard. They had been having prayer meetings, but nothing was happening, until, one day, Duncan Campbell came in the front door, waving his hands, and saying, "Revival is on the way." The minister asked him what he meant. Campbell replied, "I have been in prayer, and I just got through to God and revival is on the way." They went to the meeting that night and revival broke out. [7]

To Duncan Campbell, prayer life had to be fought for. He believed that everything warred against prayer; the world, the flesh, weaknesses, Satan. For Campbell, the tide of spiritual battle turned in the prayer closet.

THE BAPTISM OF THE HOLY GHOST

Because of Duncan Campbell's own experience of being baptized in the Holy Spirit, this doctrine became an integral doctrine of the Lewis Revival.

Through the years of church history, this doctrine has had many proponents and many opponents. There are various interpretations of this doctrine. There are those who believe that the baptism of the Holy Spirit is a definite experience subsequent to salvation, evidenced by speaking in tongues, healing, prophecy and other spiritual phenomena. Still others, on the other end of the spectrum deny there is such an experience, believing that the Holy Spirit is given to all, at the moment of conversion.

Could it be that we are all saying the same thing, simply using different words, or terms? Some speak of the baptism of the Holy Spirit, some of being filled with the Holy Spirit, others speak of being anointed by the Holy Spirit.

There are many scriptural references to an experience such as this:

"He shall baptize you with the Holy Ghost and with fire." (Matthew 3:11)

"And, behold, I send the promise of My Father upon you: but tarry ye in the city of Jerusalem, until ye be endued with power from on high." (Luke 24:49)

"And, being assembled together with them, He commanded them that they should not depart from Jerusalem, but wait for the promise of the Father, which, saith He, you have heard of Me. For

John truly baptized with water; but you shall be baptized with the Holy Ghost not many days hence." (Acts 1:5)

"And when they had prayed, the place was shaken where they were assembled together; and they were all filled with the Holy Ghost, and they spoke the Word of God with boldness." (Acts 4:31)

"And they chose Stephen, a man full of faith and of the Holy Ghost." (Acts 5:5)

In reading the Book of Acts, you can find those early-day disciples filled with the Holy Spirit, again and again. It might be important for us to look at this doctrine from the viewpoint of great preachers and teachers down through the ages.

"The baptism in the Holy Ghost was given once for all on the day of Pentecost, when the Paraclete came in person to make His abode in the church. It does not follow therefore that every believer has received this baptism. God's gift is one thing; our appropriation of that gift is quite another thing. Our relation to the second and to the third persons of the Godhead is exactly parallel in this respect......Here are two sides of salvation, the Divine and the human, which are absolutely co- essential....It seems clear from the Scriptures that it is still the duty and privilege of believers to receive the Holy Spirit by a conscious, definite act of appropriating faith, just as they received Jesus Christ." (The Ministry of the Spirit, by A. J. Gordon)

"It seems to me beyond question, as a matter of experience, both of Christians in the present day and of the early church, as recorded by inspiration, that, in addition to the gift of the Spirit received at conversion, there is another blessing corresponding in its signs and effects to the blessing received by the Apostles at Pentecost, a blessing to be asked for and expected by Christians still, and to be described in language similar to that employed in the Book of Acts. Whatever that blessing may be, it is in immediate connection with the Holy Ghost.....It is only when he is consciously accepted in all His power that we can be said to be either 'baptized' or 'filled' with the Holy Ghost." (Through the Eternal Spirit, by James Elder Cumming)

"As I went in and shut the door after me, it seemed as if I met the Lord Jesus Christ face to face. He said nothing, but looked at me in such a manner as to break me right down at His feet. I wept aloud like a child, and made such confessions as I could with my choked utterance. As I turned and was about to take a seat by the fire, I received a mighty baptism of the Holy Ghost. No words can express the wonderful love that was shed abroad in my heart. I wept with joy and love." (Autobiography of Charles G. Finney)

"Every step of progress in the Christian life is taken by a fresh and fuller appropriation of Christ by faith, a fuller baptism of the Holy Ghost....As we are more and more emptied of all self-dependence, and as by faith we secure deeper and deeper baptisms of the Holy Ghost, and put on the Lord Jesus Christ more thoroughly, by just so much faster do we grow in the favor of God. ..... You must pray in faith for the Holy Spirit. At every forward step in your progress you must have a fresh anointing of the Holy Spirit through faith." (Lectures on Revivals by Charles G. Finney)

"The baptism with the Holy Spirit is a definite experience of which one may and ought to know whether he has received it or not. A man may be regenerated by the Holy Spirit and still not be baptized with the Holy Spirit. The baptism with the Holy Spirit is an operation of the Holy Spirit distinct from and subsequent and additional to His regenerating work. In regeneration there is an impartation of life, and the one who receives it is saved; in the baptism with the Holy Spirit there is an impartation of power and the one who receives it is fitted for service. 'Baptized with the Holy Spirit', 'filled with the Holy Spirit', 'The Holy Ghost came upon them', 'I send the promise of My Father upon you', 'Endued with power from on high', are used in the New Testament to describe one and the same experience" (What the Bible Teaches, by R. A. Torrey)

"At three o'clock we gathered in front of Mr. Moody's mother's home; four hundred and fifty- six of us in all, all men from the eastern colleges. We commenced to climb the mountainside. After we had gone some distance, Mr. Moody said, 'I do not think we need to go farther. Let us stop here. I can see no reason why we should not kneel down here now and ask God that the Holy Spirit may fall on us as definitely as he fell on the Apostles at Pentecost. Let us pray.' We knelt down on the ground; some of us lay on our faces on the pine-needles. The Holy Ghost fell upon us. It was a wonderful hour. There are many who will never forget it." (The Person and Work of the Holy Spirit by R. A. Torrey)

"The glorified Christ is He who baptizes with the Holy Spirit. When the Lord Jesus Himself was baptized with the Spirit, it was because He had humbled Himself and offered Himself to take part in John's baptism of repentance, a baptism for sinners, in Jordan. Even so, when he took upon Himself the work of redemption, He received the Holy Spirit to fit Him for His work from that hour till on the cross He offered Himself without spot to God. Do you desire that this glorified Christ should baptize you with the Holy Spirit? Offer yourself then to Him for His service, to further His great work of making known to sinners the love of the Father. God help us to understand what a great thing it is to receive the Holy Spirit with power from the glorified Jesus. Have you laid hold of it? The abundant life is neither more nor less than the full life of Christ as the crucified, the risen, the glorified One, who baptizes with the Holy Ghost, and reveals Himself in our hearts and lives, as Lord of all within us." (The Prayer-Life by Andrew Murray)

"I have written and preached much on the Holy Spirit, for the knowledge of Him has been the most vital fact of my experience. I owe everything to the gift of Pentecost. I came across a prophet, heard a testimony, and set out to seek I knew not what. I knew that it was a bigger thing and a deeper need than I had ever known. It came along the line of duty, and I entered in through a crisis of obedience. When it came, I could not explain what had happened, but I was aware of things unspeakable and full of glory. Some results were immediate. There came into my soul a deep peace, a thrilling joy, and a new sense of power. My mind was quickened. I felt that I had received a new faculty of understanding. Every power was alert. Either illumination took the place of logic, or reason became intuitive. My bodily powers also were quickened. There was a new sense of spring and vitality, a new power of endurance, and a strong man's exhilaration in big things. Things began to happen. What we had failed to do by strenuous endeavor came to pass without labor. It was as when the Lord Jesus stepped into the boat that with all their rowing had made no progress, immediately the ship was at the land whither they went. It was gloriously wonderful." (Dr. Samuel Chadwick, of Cliff College, England)

"The great Moravian Pentecost was not a shower of blessing

out of a cloudless sky. It did come suddenly, as suddenly as the blessing of its greater predecessor in Jerusalem, when the Christian Church was born. Yet, for long there had been signs of abundance of rain, though many recognized them not. In short, the blessing of the 13th of August, 1727, was diligently and earnestly prepared for. We know of no annals of Church history which evidence greater desire for an outpouring of the Holy Spirit and more patient and persistent effort in that direction than those of our own Church between the years 1725 and 1727. Two distinct lines of preparation and spiritual effort for the blessing are evident. One was prayer; the other was individual work with individuals. We are told that men and women met for prayer and praise at one another's homes and the Church of Berthelsdorf was crowded out. Then the Spirit came in great power. Then the entire company experienced the blessing at one and the same time." (The Moravian by Dr. J. Kenneth Pfohl)

"Before we go to our knees to receive the baptism of fire, let me beg of you to see to it that your souls are in harmony with the will and purpose of the Holy Spirit whom you seek. See to it that the channel of communication, by which the baptism of the Holy Spirit must be received, be kept open......Destroy your idols and hindrances and stoppages with an everlasting destruction. Let there be free communication between you and God. Let all go, and you shall be flooded before you rise from your knees; the world shall feel the power of it, and God shall have all the glory." (Salvation Soldiery by William Booth)

On this subject of the baptism, or filling of the Holy Spirit, I will never forget listening to Dr. Vance Havner preaching over thirty years ago. Dr. Havner was preaching a message, entitled, "How to be Filled with the Holy Spirit." In the course of that message he said, "When you talk about the filling of the Holy Spirit, Baptists are so afraid of getting caught out on a limb, that they won't even get up the tree." He continued by saying, "We argue more over the terminology, than we enjoy the experience." Whatever you call it, we all need it in our lives!

Duncan Campbell had two defining moments in his life. The first was soon after being severely wounded on the battlefield in France during World War I. A Canadian cavalryman picked him up, threw him across the horse's back and began racing toward a first-aid station. On the back of the horse, Campbell prayed, "O, God! Make me as holy as a saved sinner can be." In that moment Campbell felt himself baptized in the Holy Ghost. He sometimes referred to this as a "baptism of the Holy Ghost", other times as "the fulness of the Holy Spirit", at other times, "full salvation."

The other defining moment in his life was after years of living in a barren wilderness. Campbell served for years as a pastor without the fulness of the Holy Spirit. Then, in his upstairs study, in the manse at Falkirk, he came back to a fullness of the Holy Spirit, and his life was never the same.

What was this baptism of the Holy Ghost in which Duncan Campbell believed? Was it manifestations, gifts, phenomena? No! Campbell said, "You ask me if I spoke in tongues. No! I never heard anybody speak in tongues or exercise that gift in the Hebrides. Personally, I know nothing at all about it myself, but, bless God, I know the baptism!" [8]

To Duncan Campbell, the baptism of the Holy Spirit was not gifts, signs, nor wonders. He said that the baptism of the Holy Spirit was a new, deeper revelation of Jesus Christ. [9] To Duncan Campbell, the evidence of the baptism of the Holy Spirit was not speaking in tongues, nor other gifts. The evidence of the baptism of the Holy Spirit was having the life of Jesus Christ reproduced in the life of the believer.

Campbell placed most of the blame of a powerless church on the absence of this fulness of the Holy Spirit. Why does revival tarry? Why does the church today not experience what it experienced on the day of Pentecost? What did the early church possess that the church today does not? It was very simple to Duncan Campbell. The present-day church does not possess the power of the Holy Spirit as the early church did. Campbell said, "One of the main secrets of success in the early church lay in the fact that the early believers believed in unction from on high, and not entertainment from men." [10]

Duncan Campbell often related the dream of a Puritan preacher who saw the devil preaching the gospel on a street corner. The Puritan was astonished at seeing this. He asked, "Aren't you the devil?"

The devil replied, "Yes, I am."

"But, why are you preaching the gospel? I thought your business was to damn souls, not to save them."

The devil replied, "Yes, but I have discovered that the best way to achieve my ends is by preaching the gospel without the anointing of the Holy Spirit."

Often, Duncan Campbell would relate a story from a past generation. A great preacher from that generation, Angie Persons said, "I preached with all the logic and eloquence at my command to a very large congregation. But, I saw few, if any, genuine conversions."

A young evangelist came to his city, and within two weeks the city was aflame with God. The young evangelist had no academic qualifications, no college, no Bible school. Angie Persons could not understand it. Crowds were filling the meetings. Souls were being saved. Finally, Persons put his pride in his pocket, went to the young evangelist and asked him, "Young man, what is the secret to your remarkable ministry?"

The young evangelist replied, "There is only one secret. It is the baptism of the Holy Ghost."

Angie Persons went home a broken man. On his face in his study, he vowed to God that he would not preach again until he had discovered this secret. Persons said, "Oh, bless God! On November 15th, I found the secret in the baptism of the Holy Spirit that made God real to me."

He finished his story by saying this, "I was a preacher in that congregation for seventeen years, but after that glorious experience, I saw more souls saved in seventeen hours than I saw in seventeen years of my ministry, if I had seen any at all." [11]

By the very nature of Duncan Campbell's belief in the baptism or fulness of the Holy Spirit, this doctrine became very important in the Lewis Revival. It was because of this doctrine that much opposition arose. It was also because of this doctrine that power fell on the churches, and many were saved.

So, as other great revivals in church history had their particular doctrines that were emphasized, the Lewis Revival had its own theology. The doctrines of the total depravity of man, the lostness of mankind without Jesus Christ, the sovereignty of God, holiness in the

Christian life, prayer, and the baptism of the Holy Spirit found their way into the annals of revival when God visited, in a mighty fashion, the little Island of Lewis in the Hebrides.

CHAPTER ELEVEN

Testimonies of Those Who Were There

Through the years, nothing has thrilled me like hearing the testimonies of people who have had dealings with God. Personal stories of conversion to Christ has always been second to the Holy Scriptures themselves.

In the past few years, I have been able to locate the testimonies of several of the people who came to Christ during the Lewis Revival. When I made a trip to the Island of Lewis, I had the blessed privilege of interviewing several people, and hearing them personally tell about their conversion experience. They also told me what the Lewis Revival was like.

In the next few pages, let's listen in on some wonderful people as they tell us the things God has done for them in mighty spiritual awakening!

DONALD JOHN SMITH

Donald John Smith was born in 1924. He spent his working career as a shop-keeper. If you drive three miles north of the village of Barvas, you come to the village of Shader. If you turn left at the red phone booth on the main road, the fourth house on the right is the home of Donald John Smith. I believe I would be safe in saying that I have never met a kinder, more sweet-spirited man than Donald John Smith.

When I arrived at his home at 11:00 A.M. on a Wednesday morning, he was ready to talk to me, and volunteered to get in the car with me and show me where all of the events of the Lewis Revival took place. This was two of the most thrilling hours I have ever spent in my life.

Donald John Smith showed me the home of the Macarthur family, the place where the little barn stood, that barn where seven men prayed for months until the fire of God fell. He showed me where the cottage of Peggy and Christine Smith stood, next door to the police station. He took me to the home of John Smith, the blacksmith, who was such a mighty man of prayer. He showed me the house, now vacant, where Duncan Campbell and Rev. Murdo Maclennon where gathered one night when the two pipers were saved while on their way to the dance at Carloway. He showed me the home of Barbara Macdonald, where, during a prayer meeting one night, the

Shekinah glory of God shone on that house in a brilliant glow.

When we returned to Donald John Smith's house, we sat down in the living room, and talked about his experience during the Lewis Revival.

Donald John Smith was converted to Christ in 1952, at the age of twenty-eight. He was born and raised in the village of Shader. There was a time when he worked in Glasgow as a warehouse foreman, and, he worked for some time at the Stornoway airport.

He knew Duncan Campbell personally, heard him preach many, many times. He remembers Duncan Campbell as a man who preached the full counsel of God. He was very forceful in his preaching, and Donald John Smith said he could remember many times Campbell preaching on hell.
Donald John Smith said he remembered many times Duncan Campbell preaching in their home.

One of the interview questions I asked each person was this, "Can you tell me, in your own words, what God did in your life during the Lewis Revival?"

When Donald John Smith answered this question for me, his answer went through me like a sword. Smith said he really came alive during the Lewis Revival. Concerning his conversion, he said, "All I know is, that once I was blind, but now I see. Even the grass was greener, the flowers were lovelier."

Donald John Smith told me he was one who was so weary, but then came God into the community. The Word of God went out with power. The Word of God was sown in tears. Smith said, "But, we reaped in joy. I remember all the people were weeping." Donald John Smith related to me, "When the fire fell, you would see the lights on the houses, the barns, as people began to seek the Lord. Their desire for God overcame their desire for sleep. With nothing more to delay Him, Jehovah drew near to us. The Shekinah glory of God descended upon the community, a tangible, supernatural light hovering over the farmhouses. When the glory of God would shine on a house, people would just be silent. What could they say, 'Be still, and know that I am God.' It was like we had stepped into eternity."

Brother Smith mentioned two men who had the most influence on him in bringing him to Christ, Rev. William Mackenzie and Rev.

Macswain. He remembered, vividly, the two Smith sisters, Peggy and Christine. He said he had prayed with them many times. In fact, Donald John Smith said he might be the last person alive who had prayed with the two Smith sisters. Concerning these two sisters, Donald John Smith said, "The fragrance of heaven was in their home."

It was interested to me that Donald John Smith, when talking about the lasting effects of the revival, said, "We still bear the hallmarks of the revival, but, oh, we need revival again."

An interesting occurrence happened when I got ready to leave Donald John Smith's home. I had taken over two hours of his time, and determined that I was going to offer to pay him for his time with me. Just as I was about to offer to pay him, he went to a cupboard in the kitchen, opened a door, took out an old money purse, and said, "I know you have had a lot of expense coming to Lewis. I would like to help you with your expenses." I was dumbstruck. I couldn't believe that this sweet man was offering to pay me. He opened the little money purse, took out a twenty pound British note, which is about thirty dollars in U. S. dollars, and handed it to me. I told him that I was going to offer to pay him for his time. He said, "No! No! I couldn't take any money. I want to pay you." Finally, I told him I would take the money under one condition. He asked me what that condition was. I said, "I am taking this generous offer, now I am going to give it back to you, and you give this as an offering in your church. Donald John Smith replied, "Well, if that is what you want, I will do it."

Never will I forget this grey-headed, seventy-seven-year-old man who radiated the spirit of Jesus Christ in all of his conversation. I will be eternally grateful that I turned left at the red phone booth and made my way to his home in Upper Shader.

DONALD MACLEOD

About three miles south of Barvas stands the small village of Arnol. It was in Arnol where the opposition stood so fierce against the revival. But, one night, in a small meeting house, John Smith prayed, "God, did You know that your honor is at stake?" When that prayer was finished, the men in the prayer meeting walked out of the meeting house to find the whole community aflame with the glory of God at 2:00 in the morning.

About one city block west of this little meeting house stands the home of Donald Macleod. I had heard about him, called the home to ask if I might come and interview him. I talked to his daughter, Cathie Ann. She told me that her father was not in good health, but I could come the next day at 1:00 P.M. She had to take her father to the doctor in the morning, but would be back home by that time.

The next day, I drove up in front of their home about five minutes before they returned. When we went into the living room, Cathie Ann said they had not had lunch. Would I like to eat lunch with them? This was but one example of the graciousness and sweetness of the people of Lewis. We sat in the living room eating a sandwich and drinking tea, while I interviewed Donald Macleod.

Donald Macleod was born in 1917. He has lived in the village of Arnol all his life. He is a retired weaver. He was saved in 1950 at the age of thirty-three.

Macleod knew Duncan Campbell, heard him preach many times. He said he only went to the Barvas Church once or twice when the revival first broke out.

He remarked about Duncan Campbell, "Campbell preached the gospel, but he was a very ordinary preacher, BUT, when the Holy Spirit came down, he was powerful."

Macleod said he was just an ordinary man, a weaver of Harris Tweed, until the Holy Spirit touched him.

The most moving moment of my interview with Donald Macleod came when I asked the question, "What person or persons had the most influence on your life in bringing you to Christ?"

Donald Macleod leaned forward in his chair, stared at me for a moment, then tears began to flow down his cheeks. He said, "No one! Only the Holy Spirit of God!"

I took a picture of Donald Macleod and asked if I could have his permission to put his picture in my book. He smiled, and said, "Oh, no! You wouldn't want my picture in your book!" Finally, as I was walking out of the house, through the kitchen, I asked his daughter, Cathie Ann, if he really didn't want his picture in the book. She went back to the living room, came back, and said, "Yes, it will be alright."

I left the Macleod home, drove a block east, stopped at the little meeting house where that great prayer meeting took place. This little meeting house is now a workshop building. I got out and just stood there, and prayed, "Oh, God! Do it again!"

MARY MURRAY

While flying into the town of Stornoway, my wife got into a conversation with a man who was sitting in front of her. He asked why we were coming to the Isle of Lewis. Nancy told him about the research I was doing for a book on the Lewis Revival. The man's name was George Murray. He was a detective with the police force on the Island of Lewis. George said I should interview his mother, Mary, who was saved during the Lewis Revival.

That night, the telephone rang in our hotel room. It was George Murray calling to tell me he had talked to his mother, and she would be glad to talk to me. I phoned and made an appointment to go to her home.

When I arrived at the Murray home, I met Mary, her husband, Alexander, and their daughter. Of course, the first thing, would I eat with them, and have a bit of tea?

It turned out that Mary was not converted in the Lewis Revival of 1949-53, but was saved in the revival of 1939. There are some who say the revival of 1939 was more powerful than that of 1949- 53. The revival of 1939 was short-lived because World War II started, and most of the young people left, to go to war.

Mary Murray was born in the village of Shader. In fact, she grew up just across the street from Donald John Smith and his family. Mary was born in 1924, and was saved in 1939, at the age of fifteen.

When World War II began, Mary went to the mainland of Scotland, working as a nurse during the war. She came back a few times during the revival of 1949-53, attended the Barvas Church, and heard Duncan Campbell preach several times. Mary mentioned that he was a wonderful preacher.

Mary grew up in a Christian home, went to church all the time. Next door to her home lived a godly man named, Roderick Martin. Mary said she watched this man as she grew up, and he had a great influence on her life.

Before her conversion to Christ, Mary would go to church services. After the church services, the people would go to a home for prayer meetings. Mary said she would always get right behind John Smith, the blacksmith, as they would walk to the home. She wanted to hear John Smith discussing the church service.

Mary mentioned an item that was very thrilling to me. The Sunday World War II broke out, there were nineteen new converts to Christ in the Carloway Church. The people knew war had begun. At the close of the service that day in the Carloway Church, the people began to pray. Mary said it was a fact that the cloth on the pews was wet with tears that day, as people wept over the new converts, and what was coming in the days ahead, because of the war.

Mary's husband, Alex, was a gracious, sweet man. He was converted to Christ at the age of forty-nine. The love of Christ just filled the whole house while I was there. When I asked Mary what lasting effects the revival had on her life, she said, "Two things; God's love, and I am upheld in His love."

I am so grateful the Dear Lord gave me the divine appointment to sit down and talk with Alex and Mary Murray.

DONALD SMITH

Although Donald Smith was not converted during the Lewis Revival of 1949-53, I thought my visit with him was of such interest that it should be included in these writings.

Donald Smith is not old enough to have been saved during the Lewis Revival. Today, he is an active member of the Barvas Church. He and his wife, Chrissanna, live in Barvas, and operate a business in Stornoway.

The night I attended church services at Barvas, Donald was there. My first encounter with Donald was when he prayed that night in church. He prayed fervently. This service was on October 4, 2001, less than one month after two planes rammed into the World Trade Center Towers in New York City. That night, Donald prayed and prayed for the people of America.

After the church services, Donald and Chrissanna invited Nancy and I to come to their home and have tea. They live just a bit north of the Barvas Church. What a visit we had! Donald talked about the Lewis Revival, what an impact it had on the whole community, what an impact it had on his own life. During the course of the conversation, Donald said, "Did you know that out of the revival of 1949-53, there came twenty-two ministers and eleven foreign missionaries from the parish of Barvas and Shader?" When you understand how small these villages are, what scant population they have, this is an astounding figure.

Donald Smith grew up next door to Donald John Smith and his family. John Smith, the praying blacksmith, was Donald Smith's Sunday School teacher. This man, Donald Smith, is today a godly, leading figure in the Barvas Church as a result of the Lewis Revival of 1949-53.

REV. JOHN MURDO SMITH

One of those who came out of the Lewis Revival of 1949-53, and became a minister was John Murdo Smith. He happens to be the brother of Donald John Smith, the retired shopkeeper whom I interviewed.

John Murdo Smith remembers that the word, revival, was a very familiar word in their home, as he was growing up as a boy. His mother and father prayed and longed to see revival. John Murdo Smith said he could still hear the words coming from the lips of his mother,

Oh, for the floods on a thirsty land,
Oh, for a mighty revival,
Oh, for a sanctified, fearless band
Ready to hear its arrival. [1]

The first recollection John Murdo Smith had of the revival was during the first week Duncan Campbell came to the church at Barvas. John Murdo Smith's parents attended the services. When they would get home, they would talk to the rest of the family about the preacher they had heard. The parents invited their son, John Murdo Smith, to go with them. The next Sunday night, Duncan Campbell was preaching in the Shader Church. John Murdo Smith went to that service.

Smith went home when church was finished. Duncan Campbell

had announced there would be a "kitchen meeting" at a certain home. John Murdo Smith had no intention of going to that "kitchen meeting." A high school girl came to the Smith home and asked John Murdo Smith if he would take her to the "kitchen meeting." He didn't want to go, but finally gave in, when she insisted.

It was the month of December. John Murdo Smith had already made arrangements to go to some Christmas parties. He was going to play the accordion. John Murdo Smith said he had some thoughts that night, "Don't think about accepting Christ as Savior. Postpone it! You are still a young person. There is time enough for religion and Christianity. Perhaps in my declining years, when I have had a taste of earthly pleasures. Not yet!" 2

That night, John Murdo Smith found himself in the middle of a raging war. The war was in his own soul. Then the thought came to him, "If you wait for your Christmas party, what if, for you, there be no Christmas? What if the Lord should suddenly call you away? Where would you spend eternity, if you died unprepared? 3

The decision was made. John Murdo Smith said, "Take the world, but give me Jesus!" John Murdo Smith said the next morning he walked around the village. He wondered why everyone could not see what he was seeing. He saw Jesus Christ in the grass, in the rocks, in everything. He wanted to shout out to everyone he met, "Oh, taste and see, that the Lord is good!" 4

WILLIAM SMITH

William Smith was one of the pipers who was saved while on his way to play the bagpipes at a dance in Carloway. He grew up in a Christian home. During the Lewis Revival, the people would come to their house for prayer meetings all the time.

William Smith was used to the things of God. He had gone to Sunday School, and to church occasionally. But, at this time in his life, he was not interested in eternity When he went off to World War II, his mother put a Bible in his suitcase. William Smith said when things got really tough in the war, he would take the Bible out, and look at it, but he always made certain no one was watching him.

Duncan Campbell came to Barvas. William Smith's parents would go to the services, come home, and tell William about some of his friends who were converted. William Smith said, "I would rejoice. I can't understand to this day, I was rejoicing and I wasn't even converted." [5]

Duncan Campbell came to their home to preach. The house had a hall down the middle. Campbell would start preaching at one end of the house, walk down the hall, preaching all the way to the other end of the house. He would then turn around and walk down the hall, preaching all the time.

The night William Smith was converted, he was determined to go play the pipes at the dance in Carloway. His mother begged him to go to the church services. He went to please his mother, and suddenly, he heard God speaking to him. But, he fought against the Lord. He didn't want to follow the Lord, he wanted to go to the dance.

In a little house, now vacant, just west of the Barvas Church, William Smith and the other piper, were saved that night. They were on their way to play at the dance. They stopped at this little house. Duncan Campbell, Rev. Murdo Maclennon and his wife were at this house. The power of God came down. Suddenly, William Smith and the other piper were gripped by God, and were saved. They never made it to the dance.

Listen to William Smith as he talks about the Lewis Revival, "If you saw people gathered anywhere, they were talking about the revival. And, the singing was out of this world. We would work all day in the fields, bringing in the harvest, cutting the corn with a scythe. We never felt tired. We were dying to get to the meeting that night. All things were new. All the Lord's people coming to give me their right hand. There was something wonderful in the right hands of the Lord's people. I can still feel those hands today!" [6]

A MAN FROM LEWIS

"It didn't matter what you were doing, you would die to get to the prayer meeting. You were more or less floating on air all the time. And, you were praying without ceasing. The Spirit of the Lord was pouring on you. You didn't know what was coming." [7]

A LADY FROM LEWIS

"You can't explain revival to anybody who hasn't been in it.

Scotsmen say it's better felt than telt. But, I don't think there is anything in Christianity today that can compare with revival; no good campaign, no wonderful meeting, because, in revival, God is completely in control, and the whole community is aware of that." [8]

A MAN FROM LEWIS

"I say sometimes to people who say, 'Oh, that we have revival!' They don't even know what they are asking for. It can be a terrible thing when you are face-to-face with God. This is what I found in my own personal experience. You are up against something that is completely out of this world, the supernatural. The awareness of the holiness of God is difficult for anyone to describe. [9]

FAYE HAY

Faye Hay grew up on the Isle of Lewis, and was converted to Jesus Christ during the revival of 1949-53. She and her husband, who was also converted during the Lewis Revival, spent their lives on the foreign mission field, serving with the Overseas Missionary Fellowship.

It was Fall on the Island of Lewis. The grain in the field was ready for harvest, but, there was another harvest about to happen in the lives of multitudes of people, the harvest of souls as the Holy Spirit of God was about to move across the island.

It was 1949. Faye was in her last year of high school in Stornoway. Her life was consumed with the pleasures of teenage years. She had grown up in a home and an environment that taught her about God. She believed in God, but He was somewhere in the shadows, not a reality in her life.

The experiences Faye was about to have are best described by her by a verse of Scripture, "Thine arrows are sharp in the hearts of the king's enemies; whereby the people fall under thee (Psalm 45:5).

One of the first arrows that came to Faye was one night as she sat with a group of friends. One of the friends asked, "What is a Christian, anyway? What happens when people get converted?" Faye said not one person in the group had a clear idea of what a Christian really was. However, they all agreed on one point: Christians were good-living people, and we were not.

The second arrow that came Faye's direction was during the singing of a hymn. As Faye was singing, she suddenly began to focus on the words she was singing. Her voice stopped, tears came to her eyes. She realized she was singing a lie:

Bearing shame and scoffing rude,
In my place condemned He stood;
Sealed my pardon with His blood,
    Hallelujah, what a Savior!

Faye became aware that Jesus Christ was not her Savior. This became so vivid to her that, from that moment on, she could not even close a prayer with the words, "for Jesus sake, Amen." She felt she had no right to even use His name.

Another arrow found its way to Faye when her best friend pulled a New Testament from her bag one day and said she was going to seek God until she found Him. The friend asked Faye if she would do the same thing, but Faye declined.

But, something had happened! Faye still went to the dances, still sought pleasure, but the minute she would get home, her pleasure turned to sadness. She began to see that there was nothing of value in the life she was living.

November, 1949 arrived! By this time Faye was reading her Bible under her bedcovers, and discovering one fact; that she was a sinner, and far, far away from God. By the time the Lewis Revival began in December, 1949, Faye had one overwhelming question, "What must I do to be saved?"

That first night revival came to the Barvas Church, Faye's friend was saved. When Faye saw her, she could see in her eyes that something had happened to her. Faye cried out, "You've got it!" The friend replied, "No, I have found Him, the Lord Jesus who died for sinners, not for good people."

Faye went home with her friend to the village of Shader. She was surrounded with a loving hug by the friend's parents. As the afternoon passed into evening, Faye became profoundly aware of her own poverty and this family's riches in Jesus Christ.

That night the church was crowded. People were sitting in the window sills, on the steps of the pulpit, anyplace they could find to sit down.

Faye and her friend's family arrived late. As they entered the church, Faye heard the words of a Scripture, and it hit her like a blow to the heart, "O set ye open unto me the gates of righteousness" (Psalm 118:19). Faye felt herself totally exposed. She knew she was a sinner, lost from God. In her despair, she heard the preacher cry out, "Who His own self bare our sins in His own body on the tree...by whose stripes ye were healed" (I Peter 2:24). In a striking moment, Faye understood the gospel. Faye said, "It was the old, old story of Jesus and His love, the story I could have told to any pagan, but could not apply to my own heart's need."

That night Faye found that for which she had been seeking. That night she offered herself to the Lord for missionary service. Nine years later, the Lord took her up on that offer. Faye and her husband, a missionary doctor, went to the nation of Thailand, where they spent their lives in service to the One who saved her that night in the Lewis Revival. [10]

DONALD MACPHAIL

Donald Macphail was born and raised in the village of Arnol, about three miles south of Barvas. In the Lewis Revival, Donald Macphail has come to be known as the teenage prayer warrior. Some people have called Donald Macphail, the "Evan Roberts of Lewis." When God came in great power on the village of Arnol, Macphail was saved. He was sixteen years of age. Two weeks after he was saved, he had a remarkable encounter with God out in the field among the heather. He was filled with the Holy Spirit.

It was this young, teenage boy who prayed that night in a church service on the Island of Bernaray. He prayed, "God, I seemed to be gazing in through an open door. "God, I see power there, let it loose!" When he prayed this prayer, Duncan Campbell said the fire of God fell on that meeting. Revival spread across that island.

The year was 1950. Donald Macphail found himself often walking across the moorland, crying. He would find himself asking questions, "Why am I alive in this complicated world. Surely there must be a purpose to it all. I cannot bear the thought which convinces me of a life after death."

The revival was going on down the road in Barvas and Shader.

At school, Donald Macphail would listen to other boys and girls talking about this wild preacher, Duncan Campbell. They talked about the "curum", a word used by unbelievers to describe a spiritual disease, that once caught, from which you could never recover.

As far as he could remember, Donald Macphail had never been inside the parish church. He had made up his mind that he would never enter the church. But, when revival came to Arnol, Macphail went to the meeting out of curiosity. The first night he attended, he was gripped by God. He became aware of the presence of God, and slowly began to see his need of a Savior. He spent day after day in secret prayer, as he struggled with God.

After a week of attending the meetings, on a Thursday night, Macphail could resist the gospel no longer. The Scripture that brought him to decision time was, "I call heaven and earth to record this day against you, that I have set before you life and death, blessing and cursing: therefore choose life that both you and your seed may live" (Deut. 30:19).

After the church service that night, there was a kitchen meeting. When the kitchen meeting was over, Donald Macphail started to walk home. He noticed a man, outside, praying by the wall of the house. Macphail went up, reached out and touched the man. He told the man that he wanted to get right with God. Macphail said when the man turned to look at him, he saw Christ in the expression of the man's face. The man took Donald Macphail's hand and led him into the prayer meeting where nine other people of Arnol were on their knees seeking the Savior. Macphail gave his life to Jesus Christ. He said, "I became aware of the peace and joy of the Holy Spirit flooding my soul. I knew without doubt that my sins were forgiven. I confess with honesty that I had never known such deep peace, real joy, and inward liberty and freedom."

Two years later, during a Communion Service, while Duncan Campbell was preaching, Donald Macphail became aware that God was calling him into His service. Duncan Campbell was preaching on the text, "Say ye that the Lord has need of him" (Mark 11: 3).

For five years, Donald Macphail resisted this call. He was employed as a weaver of Harris Tweed, and used every opportunity he had to witness for Christ. For five long years he used these witnessing opportunities to console his own heart as he resisted the call of God.

Finally, Donald Macphail surrendered his life to full-time service to the Lord, and spent his life as a missionary among the Muslims of the nation of Yemen.

Today, Donald Macphail is retired and living, once again, in the village of Arnol. [11]

WILLIAM MACLEOD

William Macleod was raised in the village of Barvas. He grew up in the atmosphere of godly people. Although he had this godly atmosphere all around him, there was still no sign of spiritual life in him. He had never repented toward God, and placed his faith in Jesus Christ. William Macleod said, "I was not far from the Kingdom of God, but far enough away from the Kingdom to be lost."

He found himself busy enjoying the sinful pursuits of a teenager. He found out that he was willing to take everything the world would offer him. But, after years of seeking pleasure, he found his life miserable and unhappy.

At Christmas time, 1949, while William Macleod was in his early twenties, he suddenly found himself interested in the revival that was going on in Barvas. William Macleod was gloriously saved. Today William Macleod is the parish minister of the Church of Scotland in Uig, on the Isle of Lewis. He said, "If you were to ask me what this saving grace brought about in my life, I would gladly offer you these answers. First, my estimation of myself has diminished down through the years, and, second, my estimation of my Savior has steadily increased". [12]

MARY MORRISON

One of the most celebrated converts of the Lewis Revival of 1949-53 is Mary Morrison. She was saved as a young lady during the Lewis Revival. Today, she is known as Mary Peckham. Her husband, Colin Peckham, taught for years at the Faith Mission Bible College in Edinburgh, Scotland. For years, Mary Peckham has been a popular speaker in churches in Scotland and America. Her story of the Lewis Revival is one of hope, truth, and wisdom.

Mary Morrison grew up in a small village, two miles south of the northernmost point of the Isle of Lewis, the Butt of Lewis.

She did not attend Sunday School nor church while growing up, but still acquired a firm foundation in the Word of God. As most homes on Lewis, Mary's home had Scripture reading and prayers twice a day. The Bible was taught in school, in English and in Gaelic. She memorized the Shorter Catechism. She could say, by heart, the Ten Commandments, the Lord's Prayer, all of I Corinthians, chapter 13, the beatitudes, and many other passages of scripture.

Although prayer and Bible readings were a real part of Mary's life, she grew up in a dead, stale atmosphere of religion. She went to Sunday School one time, an elder prayed too long, so she never went back. She saw men who would pray and read their Bibles in their homes, but, she also saw these same men drinking, and during festival seasons, getting helplessly drunk.

As a teenage girl, Mary left home and moved to Glasgow, in order to go to work. She was free at last, free from the restraints of home on the Isle of Lewis. She enjoyed nightly entertainment, and read books and used language that revealed her true nature inside, but Mary never stooped to gross sin, for fear of bringing shame on her family back home.

When the fire of God fell on the Isle of Lewis in December, 1949, Mary heard about it. Her first reaction to the news of revival was one of anger. She wondered why God would intrude on life and spoil her life and pleasure? She decided that she would not return to Lewis until this revival was over. Mary felt she was already religious enough. She knew there were real people of God, and she knew she was not one of them. She reasoned that there were so many people going to hell that it did not concern her too much.

Then came a phone call! Mary received a phone call that her parents were ill, and she was needed at home. When she arrived home, she found her parents were not that ill, and she became quite angry.

Mary's parents were attending the meetings at the Barvas Church, listening to Duncan Campbell preach. Mary refused to attend. Everywhere she went people were talking about the people who were converted.

Mary wished she had stayed in Glasgow. She wanted to escape all this revival business. Mary said, "I was afraid. The Bible says, 'The sinners in Zion are afraid.' I was afraid of the supernatural, afraid that God would come to me. I thought maybe at the end of my life I might want to come to God, but not now." 13

Finally, after much persuading by her parents, Mary consented to attend the meeting. She said she went to the meeting in a rage. She didn't want to be there, didn't want anything to happen to her life. She walked into the church and sat as far back as she could get.

The church was crowded to capacity. The atmosphere was tingling with the presence of God. An awesome silence fell on the people. Before the service even began, tears were flowing freely all over the church house. Then, the singing of the Psalms began. People were singing as if their hearts would burst. Then, Duncan Campbell rose to preach. He walked up and down the pulpit steps. Perspiration flowed down his face. He shouted out, "The wicked shall be turned into hell, and all the nations that forget God" (Psalm 9:17). That night, sin was made a reality in the life of Mary Morrison.

When Mary and her parents got home from the meeting that night, her father asked her, "Mary, how did you enjoy that?"

Mary replied, "I didn't enjoy it at all!"

The following night, Mary's parents didn't have to invite her to go. Duncan Campbell preached this night on the text, "The Son of Man has come to seek and to save that which is lost." Mary was lost, Jesus Christ was seeking her, but, at this time, she didn't know it.

She went to the services again and again. She didn't want to go. It seemed as if she was going against her own will, but her feet were just taking her to the church.

Mary would listen at the bedroom door to her father praying, "O God, be merciful to me, a sinner." Mary thought, at least my father is not yet saved. Maybe this conversion business will not come to our home. If it would just stay out of their home, maybe life could return to normal.

Mary watched her mother one night in church, tears were flowing down her mother's cheeks. She wondered what she would say to her mother, when they got home. Silence loomed large in the home as mother, father, and daughter moved about, not knowing what to say to one another.

Mary found herself walking the streets of the village. She said it was as if a record was going round and round in her head, "Lo, every one that thirsts, come ye to the waters, and he that has no money; come ye, buy, and eat; yea, come, buy wine and milk without money and without price. Wherefore do you spend money for that which is not bread? And your labor for that which satisfies not? Hearken diligently unto me, and eat ye that which is good, and let your soul delight itself in fatness. Incline your ear, and come unto me; hear, and your soul shall live; and I will make an everlasting covenant with you, even the sure mercies of David" (Isaiah 55:1-3).

Then, Mary found herself thinking continually of the scripture, "Who has believed our report? And to whom is the arm of the Lord revealed? For he shall grow up before him as a tender plant, and as a root out of a dry ground; he has no form nor comeliness; and when we shall see him, there is no beauty that we should desire him. He is despised and rejected of men; a man of sorrows, and acquainted with grief; and we hid as it were our faces from him; he was despised, and we esteemed him not. Surely he has borne our griefs, and carried our sorrows; yet we did esteem him stricken, smitten of God, and afflicted, but he was wounded for our transgressions, he was bruised for our iniquities; the chastisement of our peace was upon him; and with his stripes we are healed" (Isaiah 53:1-5)

So, Mary Morrison, a young teenage girl found herself walking the streets of her village with the Word of God pounding in her head. One day she was walking along a road, when the Word of God came to her, saying, "Take off your shoes, for the place whereon you stand is holy ground." Mary stepped off the road, and just stood there. She felt she had no right to be there.

Mary would go out in the fishing boat with her father. She would look down into the water, and think, "God made this! God did this!" Everywhere she went, God was pressing Himself on her. God was everywhere.

One night, Mary finally consented to go to one of the "kitchen meetings', held in a home after the church service was over. These kitchen meetings would go on into the night, the people sometimes not getting home until 6:00 A.M. At this first kitchen meeting Mary attended, Duncan Campbell made an appeal for those who were concerned about their soul to come to another room in the house, and he would pray for them. Duncan Campbell would come around and ask a person, "Are you really in earnest about seeking Christ as your Savior?" Mary was scared to death Campbell was going to ask her. She didn't want to tell him the truth, that she didn't want Christ in her life. So, when Campbell asked her if she was in earnest, she said, "Yes." She felt like a hypocrite.

After Duncan Campbell prayed for Mary, she thought how wonderful it was that someone would pray for her. But, Mary immediately thought, "Duncan Campbell can't save me! I want God to do something for me that can't be explained."

When the kitchen meeting was over, the young people streamed out into the streets, walking arm in arm, at 2:00 in the morning, singing:

Take the world, but give me Jesus,

All its joys are but a name,

But His love abideth ever,

Through eternal years the same.

That night, in the streets, Mary looked into the eyes of one of her friends, and saw something she desired more than anything in the world. This friend had something Mary did not have, and she knew she would never rest until she had it.

Mary arrived home at 3:00 in the morning. She knelt beside the kitchen fire, and prayed, "O God, be merciful to me a sinner." She didn't feel anything. She went to bed and cried herself to sleep. She was lost, and didn't know how to get saved. And, Mary did not feel that God was under any obligation to save her. How in the world could she ask God to give her a ticket to heaven.

The next night, Mary arrived at church an hour before the starting time. During the Lewis Revival, time meant nothing. Duncan Campbell would usually preach over an hour, and when he closed, people were disappointed. Then, there would be a kitchen meeting, usually lasting until 2:00 or 3:00 in the morning, sometimes later.

Mary kept struggling, for three long months she wrestled with herself and with God. She had asked God to be merciful to her, a sinner, but she had no assurance of salvation. Then, one night, August 24, 1950, in a prayer meeting, Mary prayed in her heart, 'O God, I love your people. I can't explain it, but I love your people. Lord, I want to stay in their company for the rest of my life, and then send me to hell, for that is what I deserve."

In that prayer meeting, a minister got up and quoted a verse of scripture, "But he was wounded for our transgressions, he was bruised for our iniquities; the chastisement of our peace was upon him; and with his stripes we are healed' ((Isaiah 53:5). Mary felt herself being transported to a place called Calvary. She was there all alone. Suddenly, she felt it! He was wounded for your transgressions. He was bruised for your iniquities, the chastisement of your peace was upon Him, and with His stripes you are healed. Mary knew she was a child of God. She and a group of friends walked out into the night, went to the seashore, walking along, singing, "None but Christ can satisfy."

Later, Mary was in a prayer meeting, when Duncan Campbell came in. He had lost his voice. What were they going to do? Campbell could not preach! Duncan Campbell rose. All he was able to do was quote a verse of scripture, "Mary, the Master has come, and calls for thee" (John 11:28). That was all Mary Morrison needed. She surrendered her life to the call of God.

Mary Morrison left the Isle of Lewis in September, 1951 to go to the Faith Mission Bible School in Edinburgh, Scotland When she finished Bible school, she became a Pilgrim with the Faith Mission, going out to the rural areas of the Highlands of Scotland to proclaim the gospel of Jesus Christ. She saw revival come to the Island of Tiree. In 1957-58, she saw revival come to the Island of North Uist. [14]

For many years God has used Mary Morrison Peckham in a wonderful and most unusual way.

Oh, those names: Donald John Smith, Donald Macleod, Mary Morrison, William Smith, John Murdo Smith, William Macleod, Donald Macphail, Mary Morrison, Donald Smith. I will remember and treasure these names as long as I live. And, if there be cherished memories in heaven, I shall treasure those names in glory.

When I think of the Lewis Revival, and these testimonies, my heart always takes me to a certain song:

What can wash away my sins,
   Nothing but the blood of Jesus.
What can make me whole again,
   Nothing but the blood of Jesus.
Oh, precious is the flow,
    That makes me white as snow,
No other fount I know,
   Nothing but the blood of Jesus.

Testimonies are the certain records of those with whom God has dealt. If you take these testimonies I have given in these writings and multiply them by hundreds upon hundreds, then you begin to catch a glimpse of what happened in the Lewis Revival.

CHAPTER TWELVE

The Lasting Effects of the Lewis Revival

Did it last? Has this powerful visitation of God in the middle of the twentieth century had lasting effects? Has it made a difference in the lives of people?

Many people, through the years, have questioned the authenticity of that which happened on the Isle of Lewis. Those who questioned its reality range from those who lived during the days of the visitation, to the present day.

To say that the revival on the Isle of Lewis came from 1949 to 1953 is a bit incorrect. Revival started on Lewis in 1934, then faded. The revival came back, in great power, in 1939, but once again faded with the advent of World War II. Then, revival set Lewis ablaze again in 1949.

Questions about the reality of the revival were constant from the very beginning. When revival first broke out in 1934 at Carloway, it was quickly and bitterly opposed by the Rev. John Macleod, the Free Church minister at Barvas. He was so hostile to the revival that he gave instructions to the caretaker of the Shader church house not to give the key to anyone but him, not even to the elders of the church.

One man climbed into the church through a window and opened the building to other worshipers from the inside. One of these worshipers, an elder, stood to pray, grabbed the pew in front of him, and cried out, "God, just you wait until I get hold of that miserable pimple of a man who wouldn't give me the key."

The opposition to the 1949-53 revival, which began at Barvas, was bitterly opposed by the minister of the Free Church in Stornoway, Rev. Kenneth MacRae. He was particularly opposed to the phenomenon called, "prostration." This was the common way for the Holy Spirit to show Its presence in an individual during the revival. When the Holy Spirit came upon a person, he would fall prostrate to the ground, his lips moving and his arms often reaching toward heaven.

Rev. Kenneth MacRae wrote concerning the Lewis Revival, "Souls may have been saved, it is not wise to pass hasty judgment, but undoubtedly many souls have been deluded, many, it may be, to their eternal loss. Much harm has been done, and although there are now some evidences of the beginning of a swing back again to the old order of things, it will be long indeed before Lewis fully recovers from this fresh and copious injection of Arminianism into her religious life." [1]

It may well be that the revival had less impact on the town of Stornoway, because of the opposition of Rev. Kenneth MacRae, the minister of the leading church of the town.

While I was on the Isle of Lewis, I was told a very interesting story. I cannot verify its authenticity, but, the man who told me the story was on the Isle of Lewis from 1953 to 1954. This man told me there was a reason the revival missed Stornoway. He said God wanted to work through a certain minister to bring revival to Stornoway. The minister felt called to this task, but refused to do it. This minister walked in a cloud for the rest of his life.

Something happened on the Isle of Lewis! All of that which I have related through the pages of this book occurred. But, the test of real revival is this; did it last?

If God really does come down and visit a certain location, there should be lasting effects which would verify that visitation. I believe that the fire of God did fall on the Isle of Lewis. I also believe that can be verified by that which remains of that glorious time. There have been, and are lasting effects to this spiritual awakening.

MORALITY

Of all the lasting effects of the Lewis Revival, the one that stands out is the state of morality in the parishes where revival occurred. On the west side of the island, where the revival was so intense, crime is almost nonexistent. When I was in the parish of Barvas, a man who lives in that community told me that, for seven years after the revival, the local policeman received no calls of any kind. Can you imagine that? No reports of any crime for seven years. Piles of peat sit, drying beside the roads. No one would even think of stealing them. Large bales of Harris Tweed sit beside roads, waiting to be picked up by vans, but no one would dream of stealing them.

The manager of the hotel, where I staying in Stornoway, told me that no one on the Isle of Lewis locks their cars, nor their houses. This is one of the evidences of revival; it makes a difference in the lives of people in the area of morality.

When revival came to Lewis, another aspect of its morality was the closing of the drinking houses. No one ordered them closed!. No law was passed! No temperance organizations were organized! They closed for lack of business. During the time of the Lewis Revival, the only authorized, lawful drinking establishments on the Isle of Lewis was in the town of Stornoway. In the villages there were illegal drinking houses. When the fire of God fell on the village of Arnol, the drinking house in the village closed within twenty-four hours, and never opened again. A few years after the revival, Duncan Campbell was visiting Arnol. An old man took him to a boarded-up building. The old man said, "This was the drinking house in Arnol. It closed the day after God came to Arnol, and has never opened again. Ten of the young men who frequented this drinking house now frequent the prayer meeting."

The revival also made a difference in the morality of the home. Think about those things which take so much of the time of the average pastor in America; the break-up of marriages, divorce, premarital sex, adultery, drugs. These things are completely unknown among the Christians of the Isle of Lewis. Divorce is nonexistent. Immorality is unthinkable.

A PURE CHURCH

I served as a Southern Baptist Pastor in America for forty-two years. The figures may change, but the average Southern Baptist Church might have statistics such as this: 3,000 church members, 1,500 resident members, 400 who attend on Sunday morning services. A church in America may be larger, or smaller, but the percentages will be about the same.

Not so on the Isle of Lewis. The church on Lewis is a pure church. It is understood by everyone that no one comes forward to the Lord's Table at Communion who has not had a real experience of the grace of God, through our Lord Jesus Christ.

There are no nominal members in the churches of Lewis. There is no such thing as an inactive member. If the minister of a church on Lewis tells you there are 150 members of the church, he means there are 150 faithful, committed, born again members of that church.

There were cases of backsliding, but they were so very few when compared to the numbers to who were converted to Christ. Rev. James Murray MacKay, minister of the Barvas Church at the time of the Lewis Revival, wrote, "There are more than one hundred souls in this parish whose hearts God has graciously touched since the movement started. God is maintaining them all; not one of them has gone back. These lambs of grace are shepherded and nursed with tender, loving-kindness by the Lord's people who have a loving care for them. This may be said of the lambs; their daily living is fragrant, their fellowship blessed, their love vital and glowing, as beautiful a progeny of grace as one has ever seen. Many of them are staunchly upholding the cause of Christ in their own home areas; but there are some of them who are now scattered here and there throughout the world." [2]

In this day in which we live, with our study courses, seminars, growth clinics, discipleship training, etc., it is interesting to take note of the feelings of Duncan Campbell about the follow-up of new converts. Campbell believed that a soul that is born again of the Spirit of God and brought into a saving relationship with Jesus Christ, did not require follow-up. Campbell just simply believed they were not followed up; they just followed, according to the Scripture, "My sheep hear My voice, and I know them, and they follow me" (John 10:27).

This lasting effect of the Lewis Revival gives power to the church. This lasting effect puts meaning into the new birth and church membership.

FREE-WILL GIVING

The giving of offerings in the churches of Lewis is radically different than churches in the rest of the United Kingdom. One minister did some calculations on this matter and found that giving in the Barvas Church was about five or six times higher than in mainland churches in Scotland. He went on to say that this comparison was difficult because the standard of living on the mainland was at least three or four times higher than that in Barvas. So, that would mean the giving in Barvas would be at least ten times higher than giving on the mainland. [3]

When the Holy Spirit comes upon a people in power, it opens their hearts to freely give. The Christians on the Isle of Lewis have learned this, and know this. They give with a heart of love.

FULL-TIME CHRISTIAN SERVICE

In the churches on Lewis where the revival did come, the number of young men and women who went out across the world into full-time Christian service is absolutely phenomenal, unheard of in the Christian world. Many of these young men became ministers, and many young men and women became missionaries.

While I was on the Isle of Lewis, an elder in the church at Barvas gave me these figures; out of the Lewis Revival of 1949-53, there came, just from the Parish of Barvas, twenty-two ministers and eleven missionaries. When you understand how small the village of Barvas is, these figures boggle the mind.

Did this last? In the thirty years following the Lewis Revival, sixteen percent of the membership of the churches entered full-time Christian service. That means that a church with a membership of one hundred would have sixteen go into full-time Christian work.

When you calculate those figures into the churches of America, the figures become all the more astounding. In a church with a membership of one thousand, one hundred and sixty would enter full-time Christian work, or a church with a membership of three thousand would have four hundred and eighty of its young men and women going out across the world to proclaim the goods news of Jesus Christ.

This continued through the years. The little village of Shader saw six of its young men and women go out in full-time Christian service from 1977 to 1987.

A CONTINUAL ANOINTING OF THE HOLY SPIRIT

Individual lives and whole communities were changed by the Lewis Revival. In an article in the newspaper, 'The Stornoway Gazette", it says, "More are attending the prayer meetings in Lewis today than attended public worship on the Sabbath before the outbreak of this revival."

The social ills of society were swept away like when a flood comes raging down the street. Men and women take seriously their walk with God. Men, women and young people would gather at prayer meetings. Many prayer meetings were organized and conducted in a community by young people.

Duncan Campbell said, "At a conference of ministers recently I discovered this: I put a question to them, how are things in your different parishes, in your respective districts; how are the young converts getting on? Of the hundreds that professed during the gracious first wave of the Holy Spirit, right up until that visit of mine to this particular district, only four young women have ceased to attend the prayer meetings, only four of the hundreds that came to know Jesus Christ." [4]

This is something far more than organization, more captivating than planning, more fulfilling than a new approach. This is God at work, and God is still working on the Isle of Lewis.

When I was on the Isle of Lewis, I had three people from the Barvas Church tell me, "We need it again!" We talked about the revival of 1949-53, its glory, the awesome presence of God, the thrilling sight of hundreds coming to Christ, and, these dear people saying, "We want to see it again!"

A few months ago, Mary Peckham was in Barvas for prayer meetings. She told me in a phone conversation that they had some glorious prayer meetings, not getting home until 1:00 or 2:00 in the morning.

This continual anointing of the Holy Spirit is still in the lives of some of the people there. They have a deep longing to see the fire of God fall again. AND, I believe it is going to!

HYMN WRITING

This is one of the unusual things to come out of the Lewis Revival. Perhaps it is unusual to me because of the traditional singing that is done in the churches on the Isle of Lewis.

Through the centuries, the worship services of the churches on Lewis have been staid, dignified, and somber. There are no hymns sung. The only songs sung in church are the Psalms. The Psalms have been arranged in the Scottish Metrical Version. They are sung in church without piano, without organ, no music accompaniment at all. The Precentor (song leader) announces the Psalm to be sung, gets his pitch from a tuning fork, then the singing of the Psalm begins in a haunting tone.

But, a remarkable things happened! When God came to visit

this island in 1949-53, there were great, exalting, wonderful hymns composed by the converts of the revival.

I mentioned earlier that the main message in the preaching of Duncan Campbell was on sin, the wrath of God, and hell. Duncan Campbell once said, "The main emphasis has been on the severity of God; but this remarkable things has to be noted, eighty-three hymns have been written by the converts, some as fine as anything we have in our Gaelic literature, and without one single exception, every hymn has been on the love of Jesus or the wonder of the Savior." 5

I mean no disrespect in the statement I am about to make. Barvas is one of the most desolate spots on the face of the earth. In every direction are peat bogs and heather, not a tree in sight. Fierce winds continually blow straight off the Atlantic Ocean. Rain and cold are to be expected. The climate is as inhospitable as any you will find anywhere.

You can drive down the road, from north to south; from Ness to Swainbost to Borve, to Shader, to Barvas, to Arnol, to Carloway. The drive is lonely and thrilling, monotonous and captivating, ugly and beautiful. How can one explain it?

On this drive you see the scattered houses along the road, the sheep grazing aimlessly beside the road, the heather holding fiercely to the peat, as it blows in the wind, and you realize that God, the Mighty God of heaven, put His love upon this place. We don't understand it! We will never understand it! Why would Almighty God pick this place to be the seat of his Shekinah glory? Why would Jehovah select this corner of the world for His fire to fall? The Rev. David Searle said, "I believe that in the Divine Operations Room, where the map is on the wall marked with forward battalions in that divine conflict with the powers for evil, Barvas is a golden star, one of the choice companies engaging in battle for the Kingdom." 6

But, when you think about it! Barvas has no organ, no guitars, no orchestra, no choir, no hymnals, no Family Life Center, no ball courts, no boy's organizations, no girl's organizations, no women's meetings, no church camps, no church staff. They only have Sunday morning worship service, Sunday night worship service, and prayer meeting on Thursday nights.

Maybe, in all of this, we can vaguely remember that we have left behind some basic spiritual principles. Maybe our emphases in our modern-day churches have gone awry. Could it be possible that we, who have large churches, we, who have active programs, we, who are in such a hurry to be better, to do better, to reach more, are really weak, blind, naked and wretched, while little Barvas is mighty, vibrant, and holy. Let us not forget:

Oh, what a wonderful, wonderful day,
Day I will never forget.
After I wandered in darkness away,
Jesus, my Savior I met.
Oh, what a tender, compassionate friend,
He met the need of my heart.
Shadows dispelling, with joy I am telling,
He made all the darkness depart.

Heaven came down, and glory filled my soul!
When at the cross, the Savior made me whole.
My sins were washed away.
And my night was turned to day.
Heaven came down, and glory filled my soul. [7]

If the evidence of true revival is its lasting effects upon the individual and upon a community, then the Lewis Revival qualifies in every regard as a visitation from heaven. When you see a community that becomes moral, when you see a pure church arise, when you see free-will giving increase abundantly, when you see large numbers of young people go out into full-time Christian service, when you see glorious hymns being composed, when you see the continual anointing of the Holy Spirit upon His people, then you can say, "That is truly God!"

CHAPTER THIRTEEN

After Lewis

The Lewis Revival began to subside in its intensity. It was not that the revival just stopped, but it began to fade in its intense glory. Duncan Campbell had been invited to come to Barvas for ten days, he ended up staying for almost three years.

During the course of researching this book, I have been asked on four or five occasions, "Why did the revival stop? Why didn't it just keep on going?" Allan Ian MacArthur, the young man who was saved the night of the dance in Carloway, said this about the ending of the revival, "Revival doesn't go on forever. History shows us that it comes in phases and then dies out. The Spirit of God may be bruised by man's ideas, wounded by men. On Lewis, people became jealous in particular lives, in a particular church. There were occasions where there were those who were all for what God was doing in the beginning, and they turned completely against it in the end." 1

No one knows the mind of God. No one understands why the Wind begins to blow, and, then, why it ceases to blow. Dr. Colin Peckham said, "There were prejudices in the Lewis Revival. There were some who wanted it to come to their church, their denomination. They wondered if it could be revival at all, coming through another denomination." 2

Duncan Campbell's reputation during the Lewis Revival grew across the United Kingdom. He began traveling to Scotland, England, Ireland, Canada, and the United States as invitations began to grow. He found it quite difficult to refuse any invitation to preach. This finally reached the point where the Faith Mission formed a committee to handle all his invitations, lest he book to many engagements.

But, Duncan Campbell's heart never left the Highlands and the Western Islands. He loved to return to the islands to preach the gospel in his native Gaelic language.

A few years after the Lewis Revival, Duncan Campbell organized an annual convention in Stornoway. He longingly looked forward to returning to this town every year, not only to preach, but to renew old acquaintances.

Every year, when he would return to Stornoway, he would always make time to visit the "Praying Men of Barvas." These men, who had meant so much to his life, never lost their vision. They kept on praying, not only for Barvas, but for the world.

One day Duncan Campbell went to the home of one of these praying men, a butcher by trade. He found the man in his barn, praying for Greece. Duncan Campbell asked the butcher, How did you come to be praying for Greece today? Do you know where Greece is?"

The butcher replied, "No, Mr. Campbell! I don't know where Greece is, but God knows, and he told me this morning to pray for Greece."

Two years later, Duncan Campbell was introduced to a man in Dublin, Ireland who told him he had gone on a business trip to Greece and was asked to speak to a group of Christians. The Holy Spirit worked in that meeting so powerfully that he continued preaching for a few weeks. He finally phoned his brother and asked him to take care of his business until he would be able to return. Duncan Campbell compared dates, and found that this movement in Greece, by this businessman from Ireland, began on the same day a butcher from Barvas was praying for Greece in his barn.[3]

Campbell poured his very life into his sermons at conferences and conventions. He finally began to notice a weakness in his body. Some friends paid for Campbell to take a rest in a nursing home in England. Campbell described his stay in this home, "A posh place this, every comfort imaginable! But as for food, I might as well be a donkey, carrots for breakfast, carrots for dinner and carrots for supper." [4]

Finally, preaching at Torquay, he became so ill, he could not finish his sermon. He insisted on returning to Edinburgh on the train. He became so ill on the train that he called for an attendant. When the attendant found him, he was lying in a pool of blood. There was a doctor on board the train, who called ahead, and alerted the authorities. Campbell was given a blood transfusion at the station, before he was taken to the hospital.

All of Duncan Campbell's preaching engagements were cancelled for six months. Duncan Campbell and his wife, Shona, went on vacation to Switzerland. While in Switzerland, Campbell was examined by a doctor, who gave him medical permission to go on a preaching tour of South Africa.

On December 13, 1956, Campbell and his wife left for South Africa. They were welcomed to Cape Town by the Pilgrims of the Africa Evangelistic Band, part of the Faith Mission.

In South Africa, Campbell was bothered greatly by the heat, but great blessings came his way as the Holy Spirit energized him in his preaching. He preached to the Dutch Reformed Churches and saw the Spirit of God poured out on those present.

The night Duncan Campbell was saved as a boy, fifteen years of age, he was at a dance, playing the Scottish tune, "The Green Hills of Tyrol", on his bagpipes. When he came to the city of Pretoria, South Africa, he was thrilled to hear a bagpipe band playing, "The Green Hills of Tyrol."

On April 26, 1957, Duncan Campbell set sail for home. He arrived in Scotland on May 11, 1957, ready to take the responsibility to which the Lord had assigned him.

In December, 1957, great revival came to the Island of North Uist. This island is a part of the Outer Hebrides, lying south of Lewis, and north of South Uist and Barra. The main transport to North Uist is by ferry to the port of Lochmaddy (the loch of the dogs). This town received its name because of the dog-shaped rocks at the entrance to the port. The Island of North Uist is seventeen miles long and twelve miles across.

The Island of North Uist had not known revival in over one hundred years. The revival that had blazed on the Island of Lewis in 1949-53 did not touch North Uist at all. The religious life of the island was extremely low.

In June, 1957, Rev. Alastair MacDonald was installed as minister in the parishes of Kilmuir and Paible. He found very few signs of any spiritual life. But, he said, "The Lord spoke to me: 'Be not afraid...for I have much people in this city'" 5 Rev. MacDonald sensed that a movement of God was near.

On February 12, 1958, the headline across the front page of the "Daily Record", said, "GIRL PREACHERS ROCK AN ISLAND!" The four young ladies who had come to conduct missions on the Island of North Uist were Jean Wilson and Margaret MacIntyre from Northern Ireland, Daphne Parker from Leicestershire and Mary Morrison from Ness on the Island of Lewis. Mary Morrison was a convert of the Lewis Revival. These four Pilgrims came to North Uist in April, 1957. They came for three weeks, and ended up staying for eight months when the fire of God fell on the island.

The four ladies arrived at Lochmaddy with no invitation to come, and no one to welcome them. A little bus took them to Carinish. They then walked two miles, carrying their luggage, to the isolated village of Claddach Carinish.

The ladies were prohibited from speaking in any church, because of the traditional view toward women leading in any way in worship services. Because of the opposition of the ministers toward them, they could not even find a place to stay in the village. They finally went to a poorhouse and asked for a room there.

They went down on their knees for two weeks. There was an old meeting house in the village that had been abandoned. The building could not keep out wind, nor rain. They went to this old meeting house, and laid hold of the promise, "I will pour water on him who is thirsty and floods on the dry ground."

Tiny droplets of spiritual rain began to fall. God blessed the four young women. They went back to the main town of Lochmaddy. Blessings continued. Because of the viewpoint of the churches toward women, they felt they needed an ordained man with them. They sent word to Edinburgh, and asked Duncan Campbell to join them.

When Campbell boarded the ferry to take him to Lochmaddy, a fierce storm came. The ferry was tossed about for fourteen hours in crossing to Lochmaddy. When Campbell arrived, he was so sick, he couldn't lift his head. Because a minister was there, about forty people came to the service that night, but the minister was so sick he couldn't speak.

Mary Morrison and Daphne Parker took the service that night. One of the ladies spoke on the rich man and Lazarus in time and eternity. She spoke for an hour. She would say, "Listen, listen, to the sighs from hell!" Suddenly, there was a cry in the little meeting hall. An old farmer turned to en elder and asked, "Donald, is that true?"

The elder replied, "Be quiet, yes, it is true!"

The old farmer said, "If it's true, why don't we hear it from our pulpit?"

The elder said, "Malcolm, how could you hear it from our pulpit, you haven't been to church for over thirty years!"

That night the fire of God fell on North Uist. Men began to cry our and tremble. The young, lady Pilgrim who had been speaking, turned to Duncan Campbell and said, "Mr. Campbell, would you pronounce the benediction? We are going home. God has taken the field, and we must keep our hands off." 6

That night at midnight, thirty men and women came to the lodging place of the Pilgrims seeking the Savior. The next morning the minister of a church in a neighboring parish phoned Duncan Campbell. He couldn't understand what was happening in his parish. It was morning. There was no church meeting planned, but the church was crowded with people. This had never happened before. The fear of God began to grip the different communities. The following headline appeared in the town newspaper, "THE DRINK TRADE IN NORTH UIST HAS BEEN RUINED."

Duncan Campbell became the Principal of the Faith Mission Training Home and Bible College. He had no degrees, no academic qualifications, but "had been educated in the school of God, and graduated with honors in pursuit of God's highest." 7 In April, 1958, Duncan Campbell was installed as Principal.

At a Keswick Convention, Duncan Campbell heard a speaker make a statement that became his guiding principal as the leader of the training home and Bible College. The speaker said, "Our Bible Colleges today are sending out to the mission-field young men and women, well educated, cultured and polished, but destitute of purpose, purity and power!" 8

The Faith Mission College was interdenominational. There were students enrolled at the college of varying church backgrounds. Duncan Campbell never tried to persuade any student to accept his beliefs. He would simply point out the different viewpoints, and ask the student to study. He would exhort every student to keep close to God, walk in the light, and everything would come out clear.

Each Friday at the Bible College was reserved for prayer and waiting on God. Duncan Campbell would occasionally preach at these Friday meetings. One student said, "We sat trembling as he opened up the Word of God. It seemed as though God had revealed to him all our inner attitudes. But, oh, the joy as he lifted us to new heights of God-realization! There was something sacred about the way he used God's name and often the atmosphere of heaven filled the room when, with reverence and tenderness, he simply said, 'Jesus.' We felt we were standing on holy ground." [9]

On March 4, 1960, the fire of God fell on the Bible College. Duncan Campbell was preaching from the text, "I will stand upon my watch, and set me upon the tower, and will watch to see what He will say to me, and what I shall answer when I am reproved" (Habbakuk 2:1). When Campbell finished preaching, a college student began praying for revival in his own life. Suddenly, the power of God filled the whole room. Some began to weep! Others cried out for a clean heart! One girl in the meeting later said, "I never knew what the fear of God was until then; it seemed that if I lifted my head I would look upon God. I never knew what sin was until then; outside the grace of God, I felt fit for hell." [10]

Someone in the audience started singing:
Jesus, keep me near the cross,
There a precious fountain,
Free to all, a healing stream
Flows from Calv'ry's mountain

In the cross, in the cross,
Be my glory ever;
Till my raptured soul shall find,
Rest beyond the river.

Then happened what Duncan Campbell had experienced twice before on the Isle of Lewis. All those in the auditorium heard heavenly music. If you wonder and resist this manifestation, remember the Scripture, "He will rest in His love. He will joy over thee with singing" (Zephaniah 3:17)

While serving as Principal of the Faith Mission Bible College, sickness once again attacked Duncan Campbell. He contacted Meniere's Disease in 1965, which caused him to lose his balance. He suffered several severe falls.

He was schedule to go preach. His secretary urged him not to go, but Campbell said, "I think I will be all right if someone will take me, and I have something to lean on while I preach."

A man took Campbell to his preaching appointment, and helped him to the pulpit, so that he could preach. The next morning, the rector from a neighboring church came to visit Campbell at the home where he was staying. He asked him, "Mr. Campbell, would you like to be healed?"

Campbell replied, "If that is the Lord's will, I certainly would."

The rector placed his hand on Campbell's shoulder, and prayed a simple prayer, "Dear Jesus, please heal Mr. Campbell, so that he can continue with his ministry."

Duncan Campbell said an electric shock went through his body. Not only was his body healed, but his mental powers came alive.

Later, Duncan Campbell wrote to the rector, and said, "I have had no recurrence at all of the disease since you prayed for me. There can be no doubt but that God miraculously touched me. I am so grateful to Him, and to you for your earnest prayer." [11]

After the Lewis Revival, God also visited the Isle of Skye. A young minister was installed at a church on Skye. This young minister had been born and raised on the Island of Lismore. His name was Charlie Henderson. During the first mission that the Faith Mission conducted on Lismore, Charlie Henderson's father and mother were converted. It was in this same meeting that Duncan Campbell's mother-in-law was saved. The preacher during that first mission was Donald Angus MacLean from the Island of Tiree.

Charlie Henderson had been a lighthouse keeper before he was saved. He felt a call from God to preach, went to school in Glasgow, then to his first church on the Isle of Skye.

The situation was appalling in this first pastorate. He invited Duncan Campbell to come and conduct a mission. At the first meeting, seven people were present, at the next, five people were present. At the end of the week, the average attendance was seven.

There was not one single person the minister could call on to pray, not one person to lead the singing. At the end of the week, the young minister decided he and Duncan Campbell would spend all day Monday in prayer. Duncan Campbell got in touch with a businessman on the Island of Lewis. He asked this man to get the praying men of Arnol together and set aside Monday as a day of prayer. The man from Arnol said he would close his weaving factory, get some men together, and they would pray. Duncan Campbell told the man, "If possible, get Donald MacPhail to pray with you."

At 10:00 on Monday morning, Campbell and Charlie Henderson got on their knees in the manse, and a few men got on their knees in Arnol. They pled one promise, "I will pour water upon him who is thirsty, and floods upon the dry ground."

All day they waited on God. Campbell and Henderson were having tea before they went to the church that night, when a knock came on the door. The minister's sister came in, and said, "Charlie, something wonderful has happened. The merchant is here offering you his car to take you to church." On the way to the church, the merchant asked the minister, "Mr. Henderson, what is happening tonight? I have just met a bus that has come fifteen miles, crowded with people, and they were headed for the church, and it will be impossible to get a parking place with all the cars that are there."

The young minister replied, "I believe God has answered prayer. I believe revival has come."

This godless merchant turned to the minister and asked, "Revival? Does that mean the fear of God? If it does, I am gripped by the fear of God."

When they arrived at the church, it was packed to capacity. Duncan Campbell asked if there was anyone present who could lead the singing. An old man stood and said he would. He led the congregation in singing the Gaelic Psalm 46

God is our Refuge and Strength
    In straits a present aid;
Therefore, although the earth remove,
    We will not be afraid:
Though hills amidst the seas be cast;
    Though waters roaring make,
And troubled be; yea, though the hills
    By swelling seas do shake.

Duncan Campbell said he could not tell how many were saved during that revival. He and the young minister left the church that night, went home with the church still crowded with people, crying out to God. Revival had come to Skye. [12]

Duncan Campbell had been due to retire as Principal of the Faith Mission Bible College in 1963, but, he was asked to stay in his position for three more years, and he agreed to stay. Nothing captivated Campbell like preaching. He had an earnest desire to be freed from his responsibilities at the college so he could give all his attention to conferences and conventions. He felt this was his calling, to proclaim revival wherever he could.

Finally released from his responsibilities at the Faith Mission Bible College, Duncan Campbell entered into an itinerant ministry all over the world. One of his favorite places to preach was the Killadeas Camp Convention in Northern Ireland. He loved to return to this rugged, rough camp site every year to preach. He was always put up in a little eight-by-five shack that came to be known as "Duncan's Castle." This little building had originally been built as a chicken-house. Duncan Campbell never forgot the day when an Irishmen came in, hammered a six-inch nail into the wall, and said, "Your wardrobe, Mr. Campbell!" [13]

An event happened at this campground that should be a lesson to us all. There was a young man at the camp convention who was struggling with his life. Religion was boring to him. The most important things in his life were sports. One day, at Killadeas Camp, he was staring out the window, when he saw a man with his hands behind his back, going for a walk. He did not know the man, had never spoken to him, nor had he ever seen him before. The man was walking, moving away from this young man, but as the young man watched him, there came up in his soul this conviction, "There, that is what you have been looking for all your life. I would give anything to have what that man has!" [14] The man he was watching out the window was Duncan Campbell.

Duncan Campbell was invited to preach in South Wales. Great revival had come to Wales in 1904-05 under the ministry of Evan Roberts. In fact, little Donald MacPhail of the Isle of Lewis, has been called the "Evan Roberts of Lewis."

As the years passed, division had come in the churches of Wales. The main contention had been between the established churches and the mission halls of Wales. Duncan Campbell came to the town of Aberdare, Wales. Campbell was to preach a short series of meetings. After the second service, a prayer meeting was held, which lasted until 3:00 in the morning.

At the next service, a man who attended the meeting said, "When Mr. Campbell had spoken for an hour, six young men seated together say 'the glory of God' come down upon him. A great fear came upon them and they fell to the floor weeping. Fear also gripped the congregation; many were overwhelmed by a sense of sin and scenes of repentance and restoration followed as one and another made things right between themselves and God.....Duncan Campbell taught us many things, but above all, we learned that it is God, not man, we need today." [15]

Campbell preached in Canada. He always mentioned the debt he felt to Canada, for it was a Canadian cavalryman who had rescued him on the battlefield during World War I.

In June, 1969, He preached in a small church, Ebenezer Baptist Church, in Saskatoon, Saskatchewan. The pastor, Bill MacLeod, longed to see revival. He had prayed for three years for Duncan Campbell to come to his church. One night Duncan Campbell said that revival was coming to western Canada, and that it would start in that church.

Two years later, great spiritual awakening came to this little Baptist Church. The church building would hold 300 people. It became crowded to capacity. They moved to another building which held 700 people. It became full. They moved again to another building that held 1500. It became packed. This spiritual awakening lasting for over seven weeks. By personal testimony, here is a list of things that happened in Saskatoon; church leaders confessed their sins, businessmen were shocked when people came into stores to pay for stolen goods, broken marriages were restored, alcoholics and drug addicts were delivered from bondage, and people were rescued from satanic oppression.

Finally, Duncan Campbell came to the United States. While preaching in Rockford, Illinois, Campbell met Loren Cunningham and his wife. This couple had a burden for opening a School of Evangelism in Europe. They bought a spacious hotel near Lausanne, Switzerland, and opened this school. Duncan Campbell became one of the lecturers at the school, teaching evangelism and revival.

Duncan Campbell preached in England, Algiers, South Africa, Switzerland, Greece, Canada, Wales, and the United States, but his heart always returned to the Highlands of Scotland. As the poet said, 'In dreams he beheld the Hebrides."

In the summer of 1971, he came to Stornoway to preach in the annual convention. He was not himself. He was usually very energetic and full of new ideas, but on this trip, people noticed that he was withdrawn and pensive. Someone mentioned an idea about future plans for the Stornoway Convention. Campbell replied, "This may be my last Stornoway Convention."

For several years, ill health had followed close on the heels of Duncan Campbell. He found himself tired, exhausted. A friend gave he and Mrs. Campbell a little cottage in Edinburgh. He could have retired to that cottage, but Duncan Campbell never recognized the word, "retire."

It became quite obvious to those who knew him that Duncan Campbell had changed. His step was slower, his voice was much weaker, his preaching was less forceful, but Campbell still yearned to see revival wherever he went.

The night revival broke out in the Barvas Church, one of the elders said to Campbell, "Mr. Campbell, you have lived to see this day; now you will live in the memory of it." [16]

Campbell later related that story to his students at the Faith Mission Bible College. He said, "Live in the memory of it! Never! We must live for greater things. No victory is secure except by greater victories." Duncan Campbell had seen revival before, he wanted to see it again and again.

In the Fall of 1971, Campbell suffered a mild cerebral hemorrhage. He fought back from this, and in March, 1972 he journeyed to Lausanne, Switzerland to teach evangelism in the school. He stayed a few days with his daughter, Sheena, while traveling to the school.

For a few days, Campbell was bothered by pain. He thought it was indigestion. He told the director of the school, "God has given me a message for the meeting this evening. I must deliver it. Please do not stand in God's way." [17]

Campbell stood that night to preach his last sermon. He took as his text, "So fight I, not as one that beats the air" (I Corinthians 9:26). He reminded the students that the Christian life is a battle. He told them there are enemies without and within. At the close of the sermon, Campbell asked each student to stand with faith and courage beneath the banner of the cross of Christ. His last words from a pulpit were, "Keep on fighting, but see that you are fighting in the love of Jesus."

At 2:00 the next morning, Duncan Campbell suffered a major heart attack. He was taken to Cantonal Hospital. His wife, Shona, and his daughter, Sheena were at his bedside. For four days, Campbell seemed to be improving, but then, the Lord came to take him home. On Tuesday, March 28, 1972, Duncan Campbell, the old warrior of the Highlands, received his crown of life which shall never fade away.

On Sunday, October 7, 2001, early in the morning, my wife and I drove up in front of the Ardchattan Church in the Highlands of Scotland. This was the boyhood church of Duncan Campbell. This church sits on the banks of Achnacree Bay. If you look across the bay, you can see clearly the childhood home of Duncan Campbell.

The Ardchattan Church has gravestones completely encircling it. Nancy and I started looking. I searched in front of the church, and west of the church. Nancy began searching on the east side of the church, then moved behind the church, on the north side. In a few minutes, Nancy called to me. She had found it. I walked behind the church, looked at the gravestone. Inscribed on the stone were these words:

IN

LOVING MEMORY OF THE
REV. DUNCAN CAMPBELL
WHO DIED 28TH MARCH, 1972
AGED 74 YEARS
AND HIS WIFE
JESSIE GRAY
WHO DIED 10TH JUNE, 1985
AGED 87 YEARS

JOHN V:25-26

That Scripture verse engraved on the tombstone reads, "Verily, verily, I say unto you, The hour is coming, and now is, when the dead shall hear the voice of the Son of God and they that hear shall live. For as the Father has life in Himself; so has he given to the Son to have life in Himself."

That Sunday I stood looking at that gravestone, and was a bit surprised at the name of Duncan Campbell's wife engraved on the stone. Everything I had read in my research had given her name as Shona. But, on the gravestone was engraved the name, Jessie Gray.

As I searched deeper, I found out this bit of information about the Highlands of Scotland. Mrs. Campbell's Christian name was Shona, but it is common in the Highlands to have another name by which you are known locally. Her local name, in the Highlands, was Jessie. It is also common for the local name, Jessie, to be the name engraved on the gravestone, along with the wife's maiden name.

As I stood there that Sunday morning, looking at the gravestone of Duncan Campbell, my mind was racing. I was thinking about all the reading I had done about the Lewis Revival, all the sermons I had listened to this man preach, the passion in his voice, the commitment to a Holy God that he had, and I prayed., I prayed that I would be a better man, a better father, a better preacher. I also prayed that I might see real, authentic, genuine revival in my own heart. For, you see, He has promised, "I will pour water upon him who is thirsty, and floods upon the dry ground." GOD, I AM THIRSTY!

CHAPTER FOURTEEN

Will God Do It Again

Several months ago, when I had finalized the outline of this book, I had entitled this last chapter, "Can God do it again?" A friend was reading over the outline, and asked, "Is it right to ask,'Can God do it again?' Or, should you ask, 'Will God do it again?'" It was a wonderful question! There is no doubt that God can do it again. The proper question to ask is, "Will He do it again?"

Perhaps we should begin this chapter by defining revival. Of course, this is an endless task, for there are multitudes of definitions of revival.

Dr. Martin Lloyd-Jones described revival in this manner, "It is an experience in the life of the church when the Holy Spirit does an unusual work. He does that work primarily among the members of the church; it is a reviving of the believers. You cannot revive something that has never had life, so revival, by definition, is first of all an enlivening and quickening and awakening of lethargic, sleeping, almost moribund church members. Suddenly, the power of the Spirit comes upon them and they are brought into a new and more profound awareness of the truths they had previously held intellectually, and perhaps at a deeper level too. They are humbled, they are convicted of sin....and then they come to see the great salvation of God in all its glory and to feel its power. Then, as a result of their quickening, they begin to pray. New power comes into the preaching of the ministers and the result of this is that large numbers who were previously outside the church are converted and brought in." [1]

Thomas Chalmers said, "Revival is the impact of the personality of Christ upon a community." [2]

William B. Sprague said, "Wherever you see religion rising up from a state of comparative depression to a tone of increased vigor and strength; wherever you see professing Christians becoming more faithful to their obligations, and behold the strength of the Church increased by fresh accessions of piety from the world; there is a state of things which you need not hesitate to denominate a revival of religon." [3]

J. Edwin Orr said, concerning revival, "The best definition of revival is the phrase,... 'Times of refreshing....from the presence of the Lord.'" [4]

Joseph W. Kemp wrote, "The Church is responsible for evangelism and not for revival. We are summoned to evangelism; for revival we are cast upon the sovereign grace of God." [5]

Stephen Olford wrote, "Revival is that strange and sovereign work of God in which He visits His own people, restoring, reanimating and releasing them into the fullness of His blessing." [6]

It is interesting, indeed, to hear some of the comments Duncan Campbell made concerning revival: "Revival begins in an awareness of God gripping a community." [7]

Campbell said, "In the field of revival, God is sovereign, but I do not believe in any concept of sovereignty that nullifies man's responsibility. God is the God of revival, but we are human agents through which revival is possible." [8]

In preaching a sermon on, "The Fire of God", Duncan Campbell said, "God is not obliged to send revival because we pray, but he is bound, by covenant promise, to send revival when we humble ourselves and pray and seek His face, and turn from our wicked ways." [9]

In this closing chapter, I find myself struggling quite a bit. There is a sense in which this is the most difficult part of the book to write. To think about seeing real, authentic, genuine, Holy Spirit revival is an awesome thing. I believe we all should just look at three basic things in this closing chapter:

There is a need for revival in our world today.

This is a way for revival in our world today.

There is revival going on in our world today.

THERE IS A NEED FOR REVIVAL

Anyone who claims the name of Jesus Christ can look out on our old world, and exclaim, "Oh, God, we need revival!" To be sure, there are many church members who are completely satisfied with the way things are at the present time. There are multitudes who seem to be happy with having church; singing, giving an offering, listening to the sermon, going home, and waiting for another Sunday to roll around.

There are many others who have tasted the good things of God in the past. It might have been thirty, forty, or fifty years ago, God moved among them, and people glory in that. They remember the past, and seldom ever wonder why they are not seeing the glory of God today.

Duncan Campbell never wrapped himself in the glory of the past. The night revival came to the Barvas Church, one of the elders of the church told Duncan Campbell, "Mr. Campbell, you have lived to see this day; now you will live in the memory of it." Through the years, Campbell would always say of that experience, "Live in the memory of it! Never! We must live for greater things." 10

Past blessings that come from God are only seeds to be planted for future revival. If God has done it before, He can do it again. If God came to the people of the Isle of Lewis, He can come to you and me.

We live in a nation that has, by and large, forgotten God. We have a lot of people who go to church, but how many are really alive to a risen Savior? Multitudes worship at the altar of a dead religion, and a dead religion is only a substitute for the presence of the living God. We are living in a day when, in the world of Church activity, everything seems real, but God Himself.

American church life is caught up in programs and activities. We have camps, tapes, seminars, rallies, gatherings, and classes of all kinds. What do we see out of all of this? Are we seeing banners of victory unfurled over whole towns and cities that have come to Christ? Are we seeing churches that are throbbing with the very presence of God? Are we seeing the desert bloom? Are we seeing entire communities gripped by the power of God? NO! In fact, communities, towns, and cities are moving on down its freeways and streets with hardly a notice of the church. We are faced with a pressing, urgent need of revival.

In Southern Baptist church life in America, we keep having "revival meetings." No one ever shows up but the most committed church members. Most church members don't even attend. They don't attend, because they don't care. "Revival meetings" are not revival. We do not have revivals to get men saved. Men get saved because we have revival.

Don't forget! The devil can take those things which are good, and use them to the destruction of the church. Evangelism is good! Bible seminars are good! Church rallies are good! But, if we concentrate on these things without the best, we can end up destroying ourselves. We need the Presence of Jesus Christ in the middle of everything we do as a church. If we become satisfied with anything less than the Presence of Christ, then we will become satisfied with something less than heaven is willing to give us.

I am firmly convinced that we are living in a day when nothing less than Holy Spirit revival will meet our need. Great spiritual awakening such as they experienced on the Isle of Lewis is our need today.

THERE IS A WAY TO REVIVAL

What is the pathway to true revival? For me, there is no more difficult question! Is true revival strictly in the hands of a sovereign God, or is there a formula man can follow to bring revival? Can man" pray down" revival, or is revival something that must "come down."

It sounds so easy to simply quote the Bible, "If my people, who are called by my name, shall humble themselves, and pray, and seek my face, and turn from their wicked ways; then will I hear from heaven, and will forgive their sin, and will heal their land" (II Chronicles 7:14). Is this it? If we do this and this and this, then, will revival come?

Many mistake church growth for revival. Duncan Campbell loved to quote Howard Spring, "The Kingdom of God is not going to be advanced by our churches becoming filled with men, but by men in our churches becoming filled with God." [11]

Genuine revival is so personal! Although that which happened on the Isle of Lewis came from the hearts of nine people; two elderly sisters who had a heart for God, and seven men who dared to meet with God in a little barn until He came in all of His power and glory, the Lewis Revival was in the heart and mind of the Eternal Father before the foundation of the world.

Revival wells up in the heart of individuals. You can never give the passion for revival to another person. Oswald Chambers said, "You can never give another person that which you have found, but you can make him homesick for what you have." [12]

To me, revival is a true passion for Jesus Christ! One time Duncan Campbell had the privilege of sharing a room with the Indian mystic, Sadhu Sundar Singh. Singh told Campbell of a conversation he had with a Professor of Comparative Religions in the University of Cambridge. The Professor asked Singh, "Tell me, what have you found in Christianity that you did not find in your old religion?"

Singh replied, "Professor, I found the dear Lord Jesus!"

The Professor said, "Oh, yes, I quite understand, but what particular principle or doctrine? Tell me, what new philosophy have you found in Christianity that you did not find in your old religion?

Singh said, "Professor, I found the dear Lord Jesus."

Throughout the Lewis Revival, Duncan Campbell said, over and over again, that the most important fact of the revival was the reality of Jesus Christ. Campbell said, on one occasion, "The greatest fact in life is just the presence of the Lord Jesus. And I love Him; that to me is greater than preaching, it is greater than seeing revival. I thank God for what I have seen in that realm, but the greatest thing of all is just to have fellowship with Jesus." [13]

The people of Lewis kept on praying. They really believed in a covenant-keeping God. God said, "I will pour water on him who is thirsty, and floods upon the dry ground." A John Smith, praying in a small meeting house in Arnol, would pray that prayer, really believing that God was honor-bound to pour out His water, because John Smith was thirsty. A group of seven men praying in a barn, "Who shall ascend to the hills, he that has clean hands and a pure heart..." Those were men who met the conditions with their hands and their hearts, and God came down.

How those people of Lewis longed for revival! How they prayed! How they waited! There finally came the day that the angels of heaven looked down, and announced to the Heavenly Father, "It's time! The vessels are clean! The people are thirsty! Let the revival begin now!" Those angels are still gazing down from heaven, waiting for a people with clean hands and pure hearts, waiting for a people who are really thirsty.

THERE IS REVIVAL TODAY

Never fear! God has not moved off and left His world. There is revival going on in different parts of the world today. Over the past few years, I have gathered material from different revival movements going on in our world today. Some astounding things have been happening during the last decade. Look with me at the work of a Sovereign God in this world.

SOUTH KOREA: In 1900, South Korea was considered impossible to penetrate with the gospel of Jesus Christ. In that year, 1900, there was not one single evangelical church in the entire nation. By 1986, South Korea was 20% evangelical Christian; by 1992, it was 40% Christian. In 1986, the nation had 25,000 evangelical churches; by 1992, there were 37,200 evangelical churches. There are 7,000 churches in the city of Seoul, South Korea, including 9 of the 21 largest churches in the world.

In October, 2001, Dr. Henry Blackaby, Director of Henry Blackaby Ministries, made a trip to South Korea. Dr. Blackaby reported on that trip, "Never in my life have I experienced the power of God coming upon His people like in Korea, with more than 500 pastors, staff, and wives in attendance. There was a sudden, awesome awareness that God was confronting everyone in attendance. Each person was instantly confronted with their sin (as God saw it). Many began to cry loudly. Others fell to the ground, crying out to God. Other, in agony, pounded the floor or table while they cried out to God for mercy. The entire room was filled with the loud cries of everyone. My interpreter fell to his knees and began to cry out to God. I too went to my knees to pray. The next day many testimonies were given. One pastor of a mega-church said that he came to the conference feeling quite proud, but God confronted him by saying, 'You are full of sin.' He testified that God would not let him leave until God had searched every corner of his life. He said that he confessed his sin all through the night and into the morning. Others said it was the most defining moment in their entire lives. The leaders indicated that they had never seen such an encounter with God in 20 to 30 years. I sensed that all present felt that God was extending His mercy and grace for maybe another great revival in Korea. They especially felt that God may be preparing them to bear witness to North Korea. An unusual moment occurred when all those present in the Korean meeting stood, and pointed toward me with their hand, and yelled. I was told by the interpreter that they had just made a solemn commitment that from now on they would be praying for me and our ministry." [14]

EVERY HOME FOR CHRIST: This Christian organization has a vision to take a clear, printed gospel message to every family in a nation. In the three- year period, 1989 to 1991, this organization received 1.3 million decision cards back into their home offices from people who had prayed to receive Christ as personal Savior. In the three-year period, 1993 to 1995, the decision cards, received into the home office, had leaped to 3.7 million. God is at work in revival across this world.

NEPAL: In 1985, Nepal was a closed nation to the gospel of Christ. Any person caught witnessing to a Hindu could be thrown into prison for a long time. In 1985, two hundred Christians were cast into prison at the same time. Then a miracle happened. Democratic reform came to the nation. Suddenly there were great opportunities to share the gospel. In Nepal, they do not call churches by that name. They are called "Christ-groups." By 1997, there were 4, 730 Christ-groups in Nepal. The Christians of Nepal had originally set a plan to reach every home in the nation with the gospel of Christ by December 31, 2000. They completed that goal in 1997.

UZBEKISTAN: In the city of Tashkent, a church with a mere handful of believers was started in 1988. Today, there are almost 5,000 believers meeting in this one church on Sunday. This church has also planted forty-six other churches across the nation of Uzbekistan.

PRAYER GROUPS: David Barrett says there are as many as 170 million Christians praying daily for spiritual awakening and world evangelization. Today, there are over 20 million believers who see intercession as their primary ministry. There are over 10 million prayer groups meeting regularly, praying for world-wide spiritual awakening.

BILL BRIGHT: Dr. Bright is the founder and president of Campus Crusade for Christ. He said, "There are astounding phenomena of dreams and visions confirming the reality of Christ, particularly among Muslims. Dr. Bright says he has received thousands of letters from listeners describing dreams in which Jesus appeared to them, saying, 'I am the Way.' In North Africa, a mission worker in a city of one million people tried to give a Muslim man a booklet about Jesus. The man tore the booklet up, threw it in the mission worker's face, and threatened to kill him. The following morning, at sunrise, the mission worker was startled by a knock on his door. This same, young Muslim man stood before him, asking for another booklet. The mission worker asked, 'Where did you get my address?' The young Muslim man replied, The voice in the night told me your address. The voice also told me that if I got another booklet, and believed its message, I would have eternal life.' This young Muslim man is now a full-time missionary."

MYANMAR (BURMA): In northern Myanmar live the Wa people. This is a tribe of about 3 million people, who have been greatly feared down through the years. They have traditionally been headhunters. In the 1990's, this tribe rejected Buddhist statues, and requested the government send them one hundred Bibles and Christian missionaries. The chief of the tribe was converted to Christ. At his baptism, he requested to be immersed one hundred times, once for each head he had hunted.

THE JESUS FILM: The "Jesus" film, produced by Campus Crusade for Christ, is now available in almost 500 languages, and has been seen by almost one billion people around the world. Multitudes of people are coming to Christ because of this film.

In 1997, while I was still serving as a pastor, I invited Adolph Coors IV to come and speak at a men's rally in our church. I picked Adolph up at the Oklahoma City Airport. As we were traveling down the highway, we were talking about all the things God was doing across this world. Adolph said, "I have friends in Denver, a very successful couple. They have recently sold their business, their home, everything." Then, Adolph asked me, "Brad, do you know what they are doing now?"

I replied, "No, I don't have any idea."

Adolph told this story, "This couple bought a boat, a projector, and a screen. They are sailing up and down the Amazon River. They see a little village by the riverbank, pull the boat over, set up the screen and projector, and show the "Jesus" film. They are seeing hundreds of people come to Christ."

CHINA: Fugong County in China's Yunnan Province, has so

many believers in Christ that it is known as "Christ County." About ninety per cent of its people profess faith in Jesus Christ.

Our need for revival is great! The only hope of our dear world is for God to come in all of his glory. The way is clear, a Sovereign God responding to people who have clean hands and pure hearts.

Duncan Campbell wrote these words, "Can God do it again? I want to say this, and I say it on the authority of this Book, yes, God will do it again when He finds a church He can trust; when He finds a man whom He can trust with revival." 15

As I close this work, I cannot help but remember the people and the land of the Isle of Lewis. I think of the treeless moors, the peat bogs stretching endlessly. I remember the wind howling in from the Atlantic Ocean. I will never forget this wild, stark land.

Never will I forget the dear people, who opened their homes to me in such a gracious manner. I can still hear them telling of the days of revival, when God gripped the whole community. I also remember their longing to see it again. No wonder the poet wrote, "And we in dreams behold the Hebrides."

God came to the Hebrides! We don't understand it all. We have so many questions. BUT!

Not until the loom is silent,
    And the shuttles cease to fly,
Will God unroll the canvas
    And explain the reason why.
The dark threads are as needful
    In the weaver's skillful hand
As the threads of gold and silver
    In the pattern God has planned.

OH, GOD, DO IT AGAIN!!!!

God is going to blow across our land! May we set out sails, so that when the Wind of the Spirit of God does blow, we may CATCH THE WIND!

END NOTES

Chapter One: "Where the Seagulls Go Wading"

1. Encyclopedia Americana: Encyclopedia Americana Company, 1996 Edition

2. Hutchison, Isobel Wylie. "From Barra to Butt in the Hebrides", National Geographic, April, 1961, Page 561

3. Ibid. Page 559

4. MacLeish, Kenneth. "Scotland's Outer Hebrides", National Geographic, November, 1974, Page 683

5. MacLeish, Kenneth. "Isles of the Western Sea", National Geographic, July, 1952, Page 690

6. MacLeish, Kenney, "Scotland's Outer Hebrides", National Geographic, November, 1974, Page 678

7. MacDonald, Donald. Lewis, A History of the Island. Edinburgh, Scotland, Gordon Wright Publishing, 1990, Page 17

8. Hutchison, Isobel Wylie. "From Barra to Butt in the Hebrides". National Geographic, April, 1961, Page 580

9. MacLeish, Kenneth. "Isles of the Western Sea", National Geographic, July, 1952, Page 709

10. Reynolds, Robert J. "Over the Sea to Scotland's Skye", National Geographic, May, 1970, Page 87

11. Villiers, Alan. "Scotland from her Lovely Lochs and Seas", National Geographic, October, 1954, Page 523

12. MacLeish, Kenneth, "Isles of the Western Sea", National Geographic, July, 1952, Page 707

13. Villiers, Alan. "Scotland from her Lovely Lochs and Seas", National Geographic, October, 1954, Page 509

14. MacLeish, Kenneth. "Scotland's Outer Hebrides", National Geographic, November, 1974, Page 690

15. Hutchison, Isobel Wylie, "From Barra to Butt in the Hebrides", National Geographic, April, 1961, Page 564

16. MacLeish, Kenneth. "Scotland's Outer Hebrides", National Geographic, November, 1974, Page 686

17. Hutchison, Isobel Wylie. "From Barra to Butt in the Hebrides", National Geographic, April, 1961, Page 570

222

18. MacLeish, Kenneth. "Scotland's Outer Hebrides", National Geographic, November, 1974, Page 700

19. Ibid. Page 708

20. Hutchison, Isobel Wylie. "From Barra to Butt in the Hebrides", National Geographic, April, 1961, Page 575

Chapter Two: "From Sword Dance to Salvation"

1. Woolsey, Andrew. Duncan Campbell, A Biography, London, Hodder and Stoughton, 1974, Page 29

2. Campbell, Duncan. "Testimony", audio tape in author's library.

3. Ibid.

4. Ibid.

5. Ibid.

6. Ibid.

Chapter Three: "Finding the Secret on the Battlefield"

1. Woolsey, Andrew. Duncan Campbell, A Biography, London, Hodder and Stoughton, 1974, Page 35

2. Ibid. Page 37

3. Ibid. Page 42

4. Campbell, Duncan. " Tape #15", audio tape in author's library

5. Ibid. , Tape #4

6. Ibid,

7. Ibid. Tape #19

Chapter Four: "The Mid-Argyll Revival"

1. Woolsey, Andrew. Duncan Campbell, A Biography, London, Hodder and Stoughton, 1974, Page 58

2. Campbell, Duncan. "Tape #4" audio tape in author's library

3. Woolsey, Andrew, Duncan Campbell, A Biography, London, Hodder and Stoughton, 1974, Page 62

4. Ibid. Page 65

5. Ibid. Page 67

6. Ibid. Page 74

Chapter Five: "Years of Barren Wilderness"

1. Woolsey, Andrew. Duncan Campbell, A Biography, London, Hodder and Stoughton, 1974, Page 85

2. Ibid. Page 91

3. Campbell, Duncan. "Tape #4", audio tape in author's library

4. Author's personal conversation with Bob Morrison

5. Campbell, Duncan. "Tape #4", audio tape in author's library

Chapter Six: "God at Work in the Shadows"

1. Campbell, Duncan. "Tape #4", audio tape in author's library

2. Campbell, Duncan. "Tape #8", audio tape in author's library

3. Ibid.

4. Woolsey, Andrew. Duncan Campbell, A Biography, London, Hodder and Stoughton, 1974 Page 98

5. Campbell, Duncan. "Tape #8", audio tape in author's library

6. Woolsey, Andrew, Duncan Campbell, A Biography, London, Hodder and Stoughton, 1974 Page 113

7. Peckham, Colin. Heritage of Revival, Edinburgh, Scotland, The Faith Mission, 1986, Page 163

8. Campbell, Duncan. "The Lewis Revival", Edinburgh, Scotland, The Faith Mission. Audio Tape.

9. Ibid.

Chapter Seven: "Glory comes to the Isle of Lewis"

1. Campbell, Duncan. "Tape #8', audio tape in author's library

2. Campbell, Duncan. "Tape #3

3. Ibid.

4. Campbell, Duncan. "God's Answer", Fort Washington, Pennsylvania, Christian Literature Crusade, 1967, Page 71

5. Campbell, Duncan. "The Lewis Revival", Edinburgh, Scotland, The Faith Mission. Audio Tape

224

6. Campbell, Duncan. "Tape #17' audio tape in author's library

7. Campbell, Duncan. "The Lewis Revival", Edinburgh, Scotland, The Faith Mission. Audio Tape

8. Ibid.

9. Campbell, Duncan. "Tape #3' audio tape in author's library

10. Campbell, Duncan. "Tape #9" Audio tape in author's library

11. Campbell, Duncan. "The Lewis Revival", Edinburgh, Scotland, The Faith Mission, Audio Tape

12. Ibid.

13. Campbell, Duncan. "Dry Valley Filled with Water", audio tape in author's library

14. "Lewis, Land of Revival". Audio Tape, Belfast, Ireland, Ambassador Productions Ltd.

15. Woosley, Andrew. Duncan Campbell, A Biography, London, Hodder and Stoughton, 1974, Page 119-20

16. Author's personal conversation with Donald Smith

17. Campbell, Duncan. "Tape #2" audio tape in author's library

18. Campbell, Duncan. "Tape #16" audio tape in author's library

19. Campbell, Duncan. "Principles that Govern Spiritual Awakening", Audio Tape, Edinburgh, Scotland, The Faith Mission

20. "Lewis, Land of Revival". Audio Tape, Belfast, Ireland, Ambassador Productions Ltd.

21. "The Wind of the Spirit". Video Tape, Belfast, Ireland, Ambassador Productions Ltd.

Chapter Eight: "Soldiers in a Common Cause"

1. Woolsey, Andrew. Duncan Campbell, A Biography, London, Hodder and Stoughton, 1974 Page 132

2. "The Wind of the Spirit". Video Tape, Belfast, Ireland, Ambassador Productions Ltd.

3. MacRae, Kenneth. "The Faith Mission and the Lewis Revival", article in author's library

4. "The Wind of the Spirit", Video Tape, Belfast, Ireland, Ambassador Productions Ltd.

5. Campbell, Duncan. "Walking with God" audio tape in author's library

6. Ibid.

7. Campbell, Duncan. 'When the Fire of the Lord Fell". Audio tape in author's library

8. Ibid.

Chapter Nine: "The Characteristics of the Lewis Revival"

1. Campbell, Duncan. God's Standard, Fort Washington, Pennsylvania, Christian Literature Crusade, 1967, Page 42-43

2. Campbell, Duncan. "Tape #3" audio tape in author's library

3. "The Wind of the Spirit". Video Tape, Belfast, Ireland, Ambassador Productions Ltd.

4. Campbell, Duncan. "Tape #12" audio tape in author's library

5. Campbell, Duncan. "Tape #1" audio tape in author's library

6. "Lewis, Land of Revival", Audio Tape, Belfast, Ireland, Ambassador Productions Ltd.

7. "The Wind of the Spirit", Video Tape, Belfast, Ireland, Ambassador Productions Ltd.

8. Woolsey, Andrew. Duncan Campbell, A Biography, London, Hodder and Stoughton, 1974, Page 125

9. "The Wind of the Spirit". Video Tape, Belfast, Ireland, Ambassador Productions Ltd.

10. Woolsey, Andrew. Duncan Campbell, A Biography, London, Hodder and Stoughton, 1974, Page 127

11. Ibid. Page 129

12. Campbell, Duncan. God's Answer, Fort Washington, Pennsylvania, Christian Literature Crusade, 1969, Page 89

13. "The Wind of the Spirit". Video Tape, Belfast, Ireland, Ambassador Productions Ltd.

14. Ibid.

15. Woolsey, Andrew. Duncan Campbell, A Biography, London, Hodder and Stoughton, 1974, Page 144

16. Ibid. Page 144

17. Ibid. Page 152

18. Ibid. Page 152

19. "Lewis, Land of Revival". Audio Tape, Belfast, Ireland, Ambassador Productions Ltd.

20. Campbell, Duncan. The Price and Power of Revival, London, Parry Jackman, 1957, Page 68

21. Campbell, Duncan. "Tape #9' audio tape in author's library

Chapter Ten: "The Theology of the Lewis Revival"

1. Woolsey, Andrew. Duncan Campbell, A Biography, London, Hodder and Stoughton, 1974, Page 65

2. Campbell, Duncan. "Tape #5", audio tape in author's library

3. Ibid.

4. Campbell, Duncan. "Tape #6" , audio tape in author's library

5. Woolsey, Andrew. Duncan Campbell, A Biography, London, Hodder and Stoughton, 1974, Page 165

6. Ibid. Page 157

7. "Lewis, Land of Revival", Audio Tape, Belfast, Ireland, Ambassador Productions Ltd.

8. Campbell, Duncan. "Tape #3" , audio tape in author's library

9. Campbell, Duncan. The Price and Power of Revival, London, Parry Jackman, 1957, Page 16

10. Ibid. Page 40

11. Campbell, Duncan. "Tape #2", audio tape in author's library

Chapter Eleven: "Testimonies of those who were there"

1. "The Wind of the Spirit". Video Tape, Belfast, Ireland, Ambassador Productions Ltd.

2. Ibid.

3. Ibid.

4. Ibid.

5. Ibid.

6. Ibid.

7. "Lewis, Land of Revival", Audio Tape, Belfast, Ireland, Ambassador Productions Ltd.

8. Ibid.

9. Ibid.

10. Campbell, Duncan. God's Standard, Fort Washington, Pennsylvania, Christian Literature Crusade, 1967, Page 63

11. Ibid. Page 73

12. Ibid. Page 71

13. "Video Message by Mary Peckham". September 22, 1996 at Green Acres Baptist Church, Warner-Robbins, Georgia.

14. Ibid.

Chapter Twelve: "The Lasting Effects of the Lewis Revival"

1. MacRae, Kenneth. "The Faith Mission and the Lewis Revival" Paper in author's library.

2. Campbell, Duncan. God's Answer, Fort Washington, Pennsylvania, Christian Literature Crusade, 1967, Page 90

3. Searle, David C. "Lewis, Land of Revival, Thirty-five Years After", Christian Irishman, 1987, Page 1-3

4. Campbell, Duncan. "The Revival in the Hebrides", Keswick Week, 1952

5. Ibid.

6. Searle, David C. "Lewis, Land of Revival, thirty-five Years After", Christian Irishman, 1987, Page 2

7. Peterson, John. "Heaven Came Down"

Chapter Thirteen: "After Lewis"

1. "The Wind of the Spirit". Video Tape, Belfast, Ireland, Ambassador Productions Ltd.

2. Ibid.

3. Woolsey, Andrew. Duncan Campbell, A Biography, London, Hodder and Stoughton, 1974, Page 162

4. Ibid. Page 166

5. Ferguson, John. When God Came Down, Inverness, Lewis Recordings, 2000, Page 34

6. Campbell, Duncan. "Tape # 9" audio tape in author's library

7. Woolsey, Andrew. Duncan Campbell, A Biography, London, Hodder and Stoughton, 1974, Page 169

8. Campbell, Duncan. "Tape #6" audio tape in author's library

9. Woolsey, Andrew. Duncan Campbell, A Biography, London, Hodder and Stoughton, 1974, Page 172

10. Ibid. Page 173

11. Ibid. Page 175

12. Campbell, Duncan. "Tape # 12", audio tape in author's library

13. Woolsey, Andrew. Duncan Campbell, A Biography, London, Hodder and Stoughton, 1974, Page 179

14. Ibid. Page 178

15. Ibid. Page 181-82

16. Ibid. Page 189

17. Ibid. Page 190

Chapter Fourteen: "Will God Do It Again?"

1. Ferguson, John. When God Came Down, Inverness, Lewis Recordings, 2000, Page 15-16

2. "The Wind of the Spirit", Video Tape, Belfast, Ireland, Ambassador Productions Lts.

3. Olford, Stephen. Heart Cry for Revival, Westwood, New Jersey, Fleming H. Revell Company, 1962, Page 15

4. Ibid. Page 17

5. Ibid. Page 17

6. Ibid. Page 17

7. Campbell, Duncan. "Tape #3" audio tape in author's library

8. Campbell, Duncan. "Tape #8" , audio tape in author's library

9. Campbell, Duncan. "Tape #12", audio tape in author's library

10. Woolsey, Andrew. Duncan Campbell, A Biography, London, Hodder and Stoughton, 1974, Page 189

11. Campbell, Duncan. God's Standard, Fort Washington, Pennsylvania, Christian Literature Crusade, 1967, Page 55

12. Ibid. Page 31

13. Campbell, Duncan. The Price and Power of Revival, London, Parry Jackman, 1957, Page 36

14. E-mail from Dr. Henry Blackaby

15. Campbell, Duncan. The Price and Power of Revival, London, Parry Jackman, 1957, Page 65

BIBLIOGRAPHY

BOOKS

Black, Hugh. Revival, Including the Prophetic Vision of Jean Darnall. Greenock, Scotland: New
    Dawn Books, 1993.

Black, Hugh. Revival: Personal Encounters. Greenock, Scotland: New Dawn Books, 1993.

Campbell, Duncan. God's Answer. Fort Washington, Pennsylvania: Christian Literature Crusade,
    1967.

Campbell, Duncan. God's Standard. Fort Washington, Pennsylvania: Christian Literature Crusade,
    1967.

Campbell, Duncan. The Price and Power of Revival. London: Parry Jackman, 1957.

Campbell, Murdoch. Gleanings of Highland Harvest. Houston, Texas: Christian Focus Publications,
    1957.

Greenfield, John. Power from on High. Atlantic City, New Jersey: The World Wide Revival Prayer
    Movement, 1927.

Macaulay, Murdo. The Burning Bush in Carloway, Stornoway, Isle of Lewis, Essprint Ltd., 1984.

MacRae, Alexander. Revivals in the Highlands and Islands. Hartshill, Stoke-on-Trent: Tentmaker
    Publications, 1998.

MacDonald, Donald. Lewis, A History of the Island. Edinburgh, Scotland: Gordon Wright Publishing,
    1990

Olford, Stephen F. Heart-Cry for Revival. Westwood, New Jersey: Fleming H. Revell Company,
    1962.

Peckham, Colin N. Heritage of Revival. Edinburgh, Scotland: The Faith Mission, 1986.

The Scottish Psalmody. Edinburgh, Scotland: General Assembly of the Free Church of Scotland,
    1992.

The Shorter Catechism with Scripture Proofs. Edinburgh, Scotland: The Banner of Truth Trust.

Steel, Tom. The Life and Death of St. Kilda. Hammersmith, London: Harper Collins Publishers, 1975.

Woolsey, Andrew. Duncan Campbell, a Biography- The Sound of Battle. London: Hodder and
    Stoughton, 1974.

VIDEOS

"Transformations II". The Sentinel Group, 2001.

"Mary Peckham". A message delivered at Green Acres Baptist Church, Warner-Robbins, Georgia
    On September 22, 1996.

"The Wind of the Spirit". Belfast, Ireland: Ambassador Productions Ltd., 1999.

ARTICLES

Campbell, Duncan. "The Revival in the Hebrides". Keswick Week, 1952

Hutchison, Isobel Wylie. "From Barra to Butt in the Hebrides". National Geographic Magazine,
    April, 1961.

MacLeish, Kenneth. "Scotland's outer Hebrides". National Geographic Magazine, November,
    1974.

MacLeish, Kenneth. "Isles of the Western Sea". National Geographic Magazine, July, 1952.

MacRae, Kenneth A. "The Faith Mission and the Lewis Revival". Internet: www.reformed, org.
    Uk/resurgence3.html

Reynolds, Robert J. "Over the Sea to Scotland's Skye". National Geographic Magazine, May,
    1970.

Searle, David C. "Lewis, Land of Revival- Thirty-five Years After", Christian Irishman, April,
    1987.

Villiers, Alan. "Scotland, From her lovely Lochs and Seas", National Geographic Magazine,
    October, 1954.

AUDIO TAPES

Campbell, Duncan. "Building the Walls". Edinburgh, Scotland: The Faith Mission.

Campbell, Duncan. "God's Hand Upon a Man". Edinburgh, Scotland: The Faith Mission.

Campbell, Duncan. 'Walking with God"

Campbell, Duncan. "The Lewis Revival'. Edinburgh, Scotland: The Faith Mission.

Campbell, Duncan. "The Reality of the Divine in Christian Experience". Edinburgh, Scotland:
The Faith Mission.

Campbell, Duncan. "Ascending the Hill of the Lord". Edinburgh, Scotland: The Faith Mission.

Campbell, Duncan. "Principles that govern Spiritual Quickening". Edinburgh, Scotland: The
Faith Mission.

Campbell, Duncan. "Action and Obedience". Edinburgh, Scotland: The Faith Mission.

Campbell, Duncan. "Revival Tape #1"

Campbell, Duncan. "Revival Tape #2"

Campbell, Duncan. "Revival Tape #3"

Campbell, Duncan. "Revival Tape #4"

Campbell, Duncan. "Revival Tape #5"

Campbell, Duncan. "Revival Tape #6"

Campbell, Duncan. "Revival Tape #7"

Campbell, Duncan. "The Fire of God"

Campbell, Duncan. "The Holy Ghost in Revival"

Campbell, Duncan. "Heart Preparation for Revival"

Campbell, Duncan. "The Nature of Revival"

Campbell, Duncan. "Meeting a Need"

Campbell, Duncan. "Conversion Testimony"

Campbell, Duncan. "When the Fire of the Lord Fell"

Campbell, Duncan. "Dry Valleys Filled with Water"

Campbell, Duncan. "The Sacrifice that is Pleasing to God"

"Lewis, Land of Revival". Belfast, Ireland: Ambassador Productions Ltd.

Catch the Wind

The Story of Spiritual Awakening on
The Hebrides Islands

For a signed copy, send $18.95
($14.95 + $4.00 s/h) to:

Brad Allen
#12 Area A
Lake Humphries
Marlow, OK 73055
E-mail: BLA@texhoma.net

Order online at:
www.amazon.com
www.bn.com
www.borders.com

Order direct from Word Association Publishers and save 10%
orders@wordassociation.com

1-800-827-7903